ISBN 0-634-05411-2

7777 W. BLUEMOUND RD. P.O.BOX 13819 MILWAUKEE, WI 53213

For all works contained herein:
Unauthorized copying, arranging, adapting, recording or public performance is an infringement of copyright.
Infringers are liable under the law.

Visit Hal Leonard Online at
www.halleonard.com

ABOUT THIS BOOK

When playing through the transcriptions in this book, it is important to consider the following:

1. The primary keyboard part always appears directly below the vocal line.

2. Any secondary keyboard parts appear below the primary keyboard part. The instrument sound is always indicated in the measure in which the part is first played. (Sound changes are also indicated where appropriate.) In some instances, background keyboard parts, such as those involving "comping," or "playing the chords," are omitted.

3. Other prominent instrumental parts, such as string and horn lines, are also included. It is important to note that these parts are arranged so that they may be played as secondary keyboard parts. The pitches are accurate; however, the voicings of the chords may be modified to be more indicative of a keyboard approach.

4. If there is no keyboard part on the recording for an extended time, other instrumental parts are often arranged to be played by the primary keyboard part. These sections are optional and are intended to be played only if the actual instruments (such as guitar) are not available.

5. "Fill" boxes are sometimes included when a particular fill, or figure, is played on the repeat or D.S. only. A typical indication would be "Play Fill 1 (2nd time)." In some instances, minor differences on a repeat or D.S. are not notated.

The transcriptions in this book are useful in a variety of situations: with a band, with a sequencer, with a CD, or solo playing. Whatever your purpose, you can now play your favorite songs just as the artists recorded them.

CONTENTS

Title	Page	Artist
Baby Love	4	The Supremes
Boogie On Reggae Woman	8	Stevie Wonder
Boogie Oogie Oogie	19	A Taste of Honey
(Sittin' On) The Dock of the Bay	26	Otis Redding
Easy	32	The Commodores
Endless Love	39	Diana Ross & Lionel Richie
Fallin'	50	Alicia Keys
Green Onions	66	Booker T. & The MG's
Hallelujah I Love Her So	59	Ray Charles
Here and Now	74	Luther Vandross
Higher Ground	84	Stevie Wonder
How Sweet It Is (To Be Loved by You)	105	Marvin Gaye
I Can't Get Next to You	114	The Temptations
I Can't Help Myself (Sugar Pie, Honey Bunch)	122	Four Tops
I Heard It Through the Grapevine	131	Marvin Gaye
I Wish	140	Stevie Wonder
I'll Be There	154	Jackson 5
Just Once	162	Quincy Jones
Lady Marmalade	178	Labelle
Mess Around	191	Ray Charles
Miss You Like Crazy	200	Natalie Cole
Money (That's What I Want)	210	Barrett Strong
Nothing from Nothing	214	Billy Preston
On the Wings of Love	224	Jeffrey Osborne
Respect Yourself	231	The Staple Singers
Ribbon in the Sky	242	Stevie Wonder
Sail On	249	The Commodores
Send One Your Love	258	Stevie Wonder
Superstition	270	Stevie Wonder
Sweet Love	290	Anita Baker
Tell It Like It Is	308	Aaron Neville
This Masquerade	299	George Benson
Three Times a Lady	314	The Commodores
We're in This Love Together	321	Al Jarreau
What'd I Say	332	Ray Charles

Baby Love

Words and Music by Brian Holland,
Edward Holland and Lamont Dozier

© 1964 (Renewed 1992) JOBETE MUSIC CO., INC.
All Rights Controlled and Administered by EMI BLACKWOOD MUSIC INC. on behalf of STONE AGATE MUSIC (A Division of JOBETE MUSIC CO., INC.)
All Rights Reserved   International Copyright Secured   Used by Permission

Boogie On Reggae Woman

Words and Music by
Stevie Wonder

Moderately fast (♩ = 108)

* *Multiple parts have been combined to be playable by one keyboard.*

© 1974 JOBETE MUSIC CO., INC. and BLACK BULL MUSIC
c/o EMI APRIL MUSIC INC.
All Rights Reserved   International Copyright Secured   Used by Permission

14

15

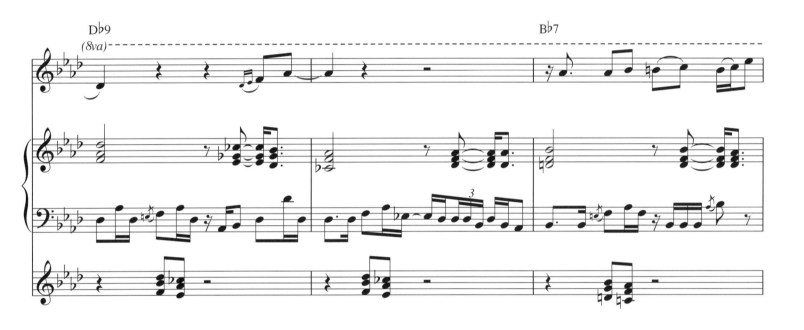

Boog-ie on reg-gae wom-an.

Boogie Oogie Oogie

Words and Music by Janice Marie Johnson
and Perry Kibble

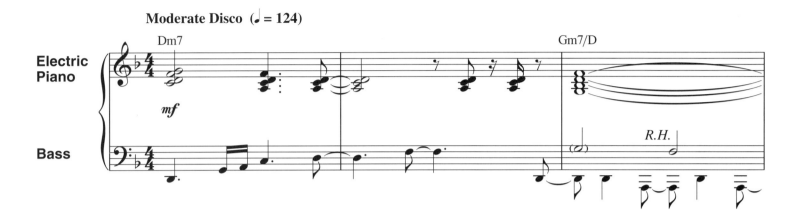

20

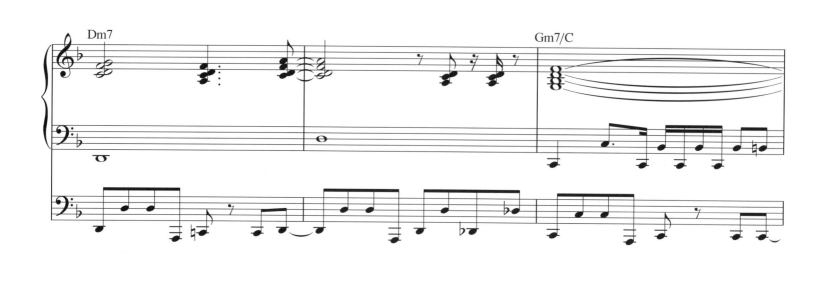

(Sittin' On) The Dock of the Bay

Words and Music by Steve Cropper and Otis Redding

Copyright © 1968, 1975 IRVING MUSIC, INC.
Copyright Renewed
All Rights Reserved Used by Permission

46

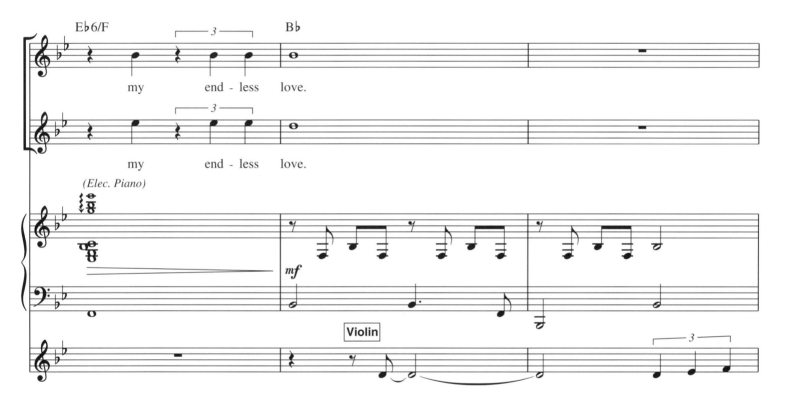
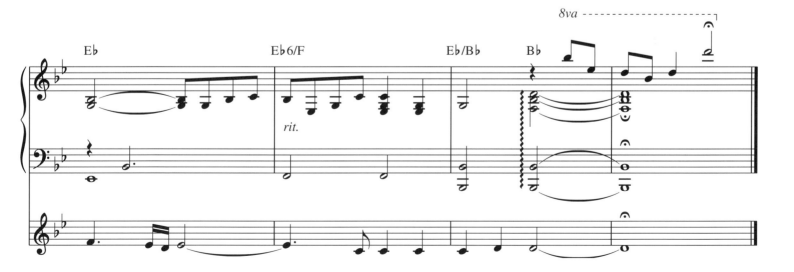

Fallin'

Words and Music by
Alicia Keys

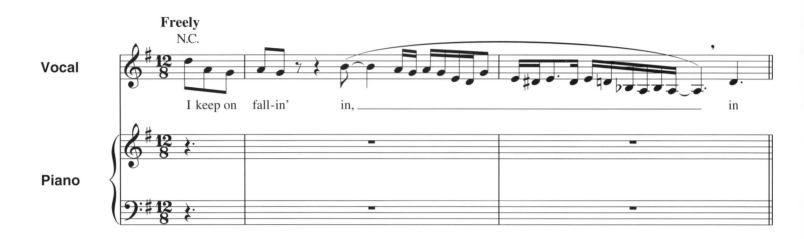
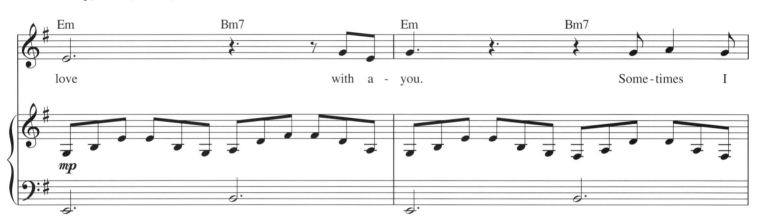
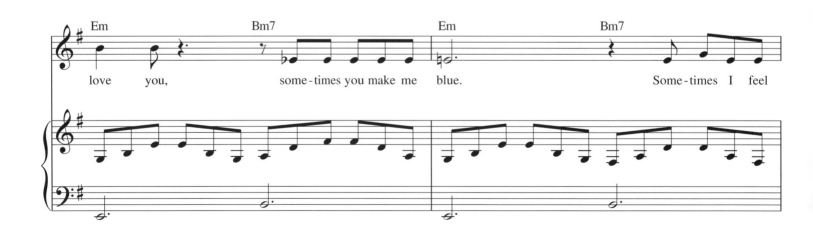

© 2001 EMI APRIL MUSIC INC. and LELLOW PRODUCTIONS
All Rights Controlled and Administered by EMI APRIL MUSIC INC.
All Rights Reserved International Copyright Secured Used by Permission

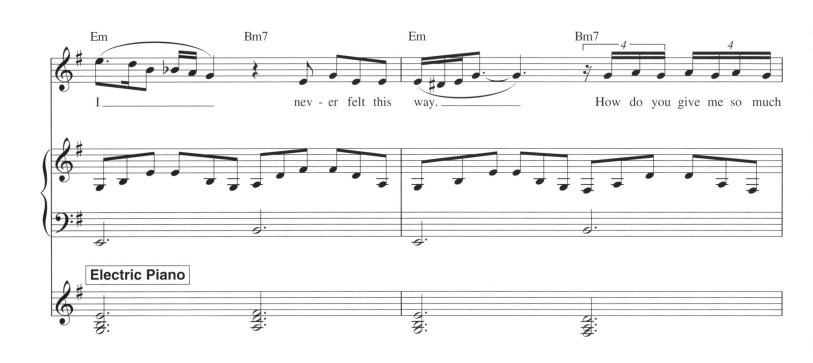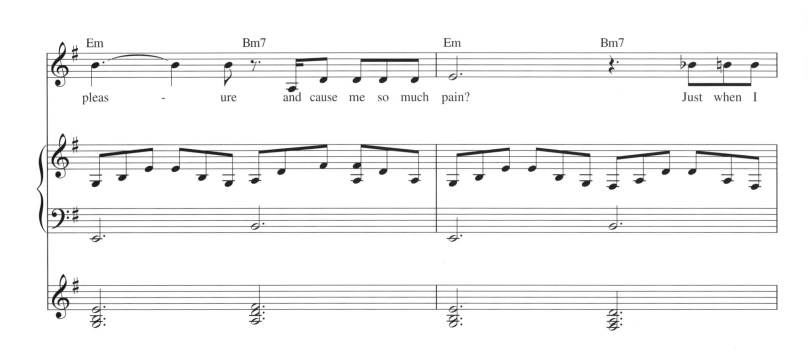

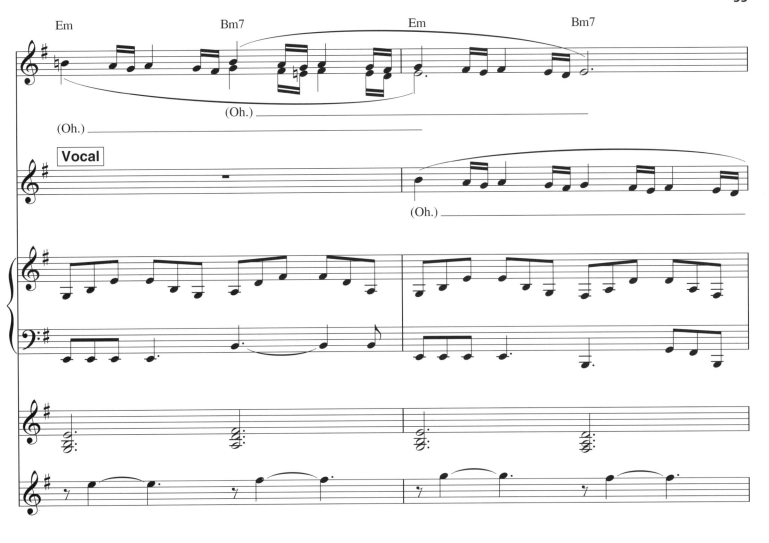
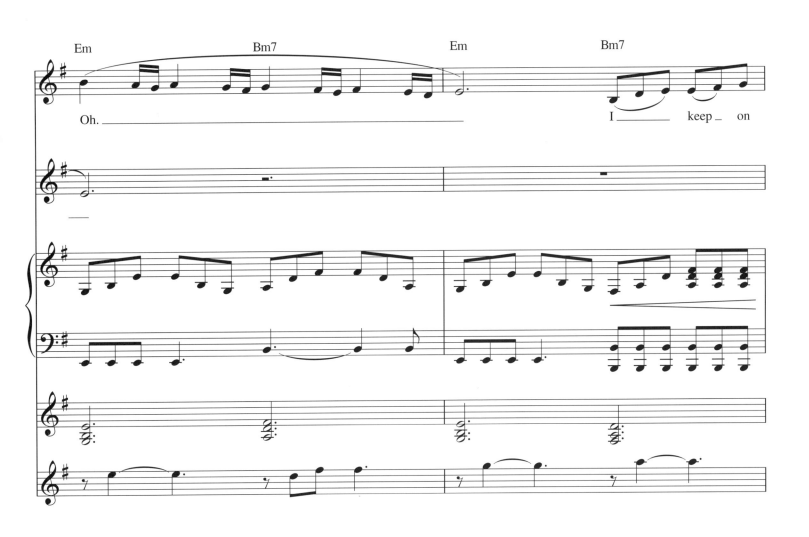

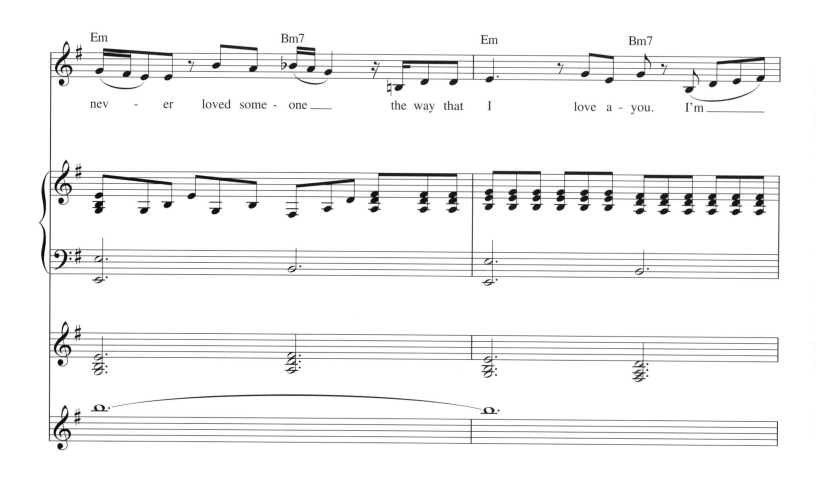

Hallelujah I Love Her So

Words and Music by
Ray Charles

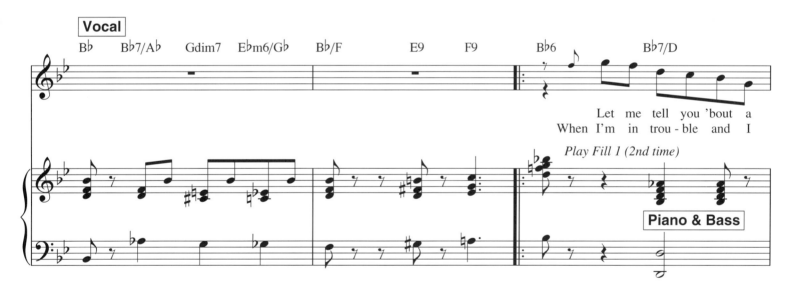
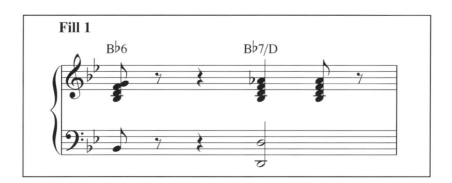

Copyright © 1956 by Unichappell Music Inc.
Copyright Renewed
International Copyright Secured   All Rights Reserved

* Knocking sound

Green Onions

Written by Al Jackson, Jr., Lewis Steinberg,
Booker T. Jones and Steve Cropper

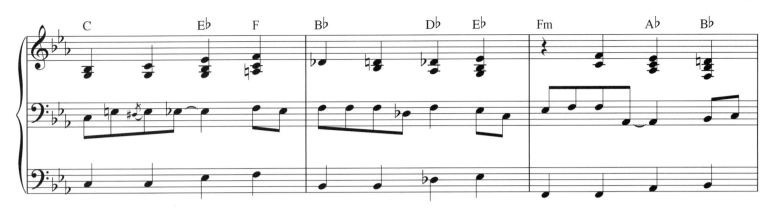
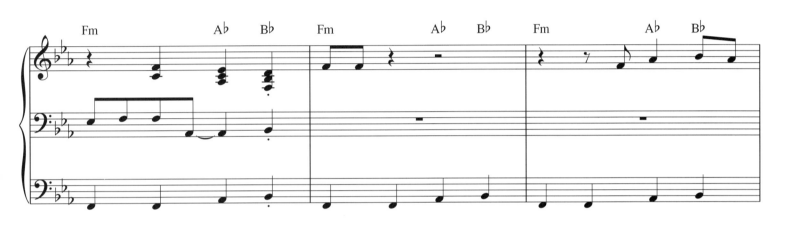
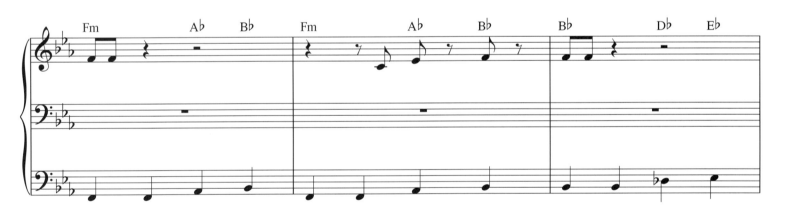

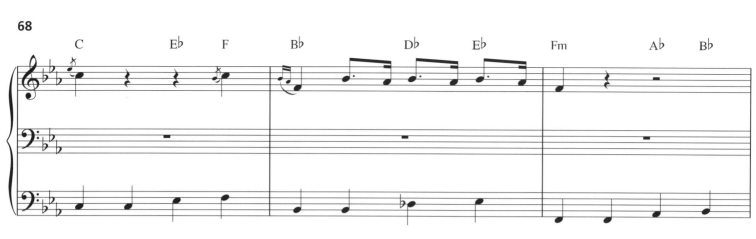

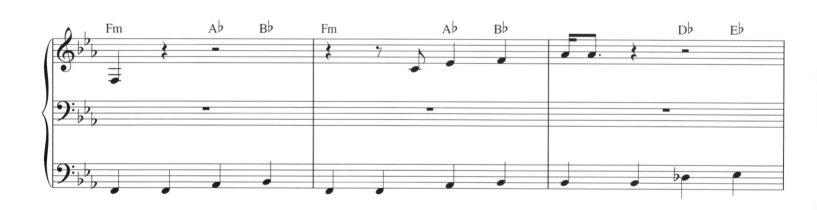

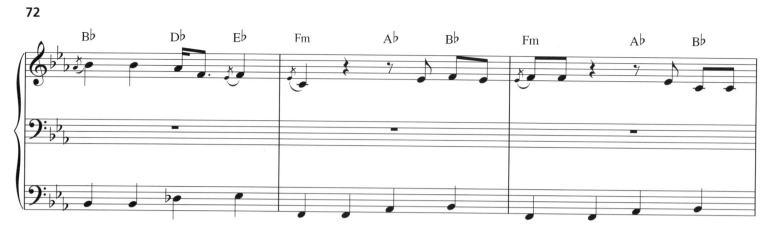

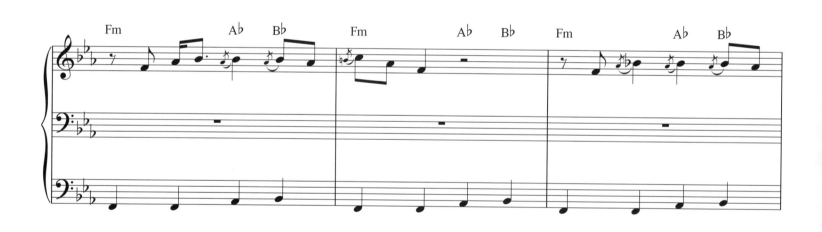
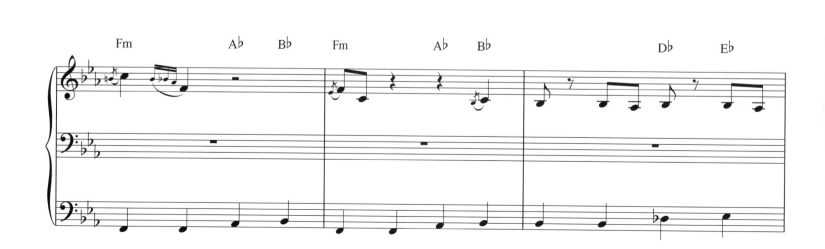

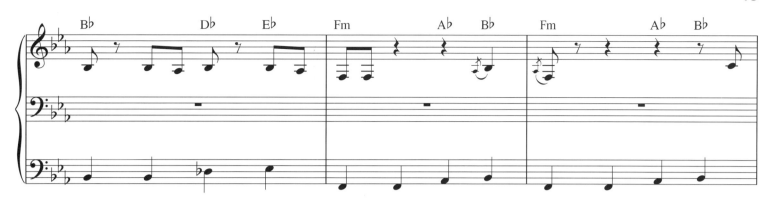
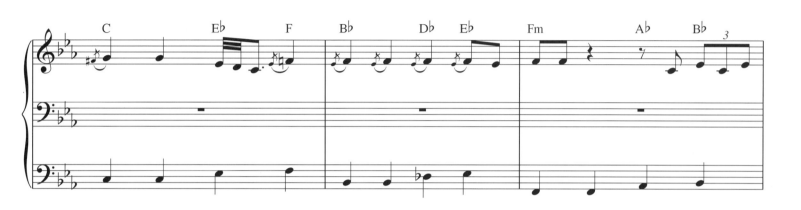

Here and Now

Words and Music by Terry Steele
and David Elliot

© 1989 EMI APRIL MUSIC INC., OLLIE BROWN SUGAR MUSIC, UNIVERSAL - MCA MUSIC PUBLISHING, A Division of UNIVERSAL STUDIOS, INC. and D.L.E. MUSIC
All Rights for OLLIE BROWN SUGAR MUSIC throughout the World Controlled and Administered by EMI APRIL MUSIC INC.
All Rights for D.L.E. MUSIC in the U.S. and Canada Controlled and Administered by UNIVERSAL - MCA MUSIC PUBLISHING, A Division of UNIVERSAL STUDIOS, INC.
All Rights for D.L.E. MUSIC in the World excluding the U.S. and Canada Controlled and Administered by EMI APRIL MUSIC INC.
All Rights Reserved   International Copyright Secured   Used by Permission

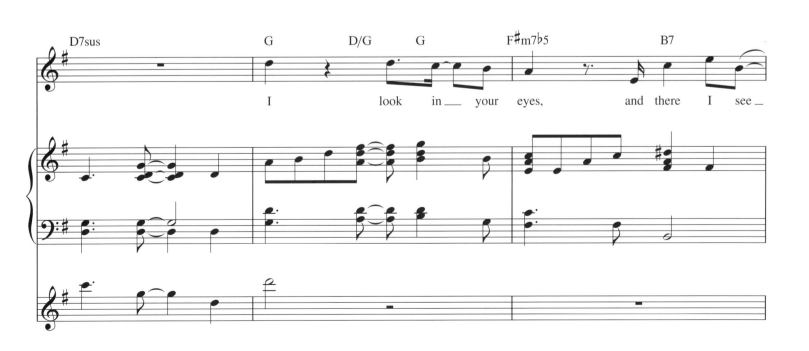

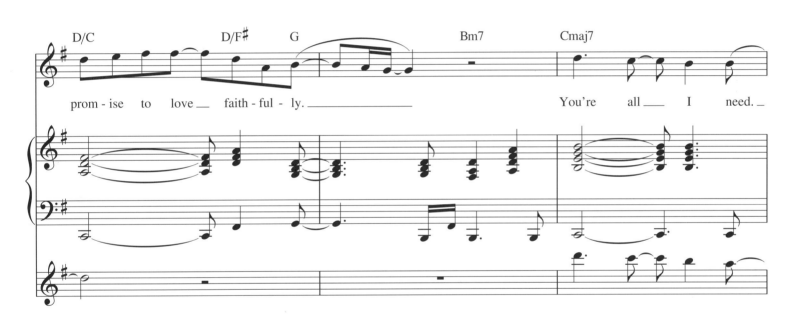

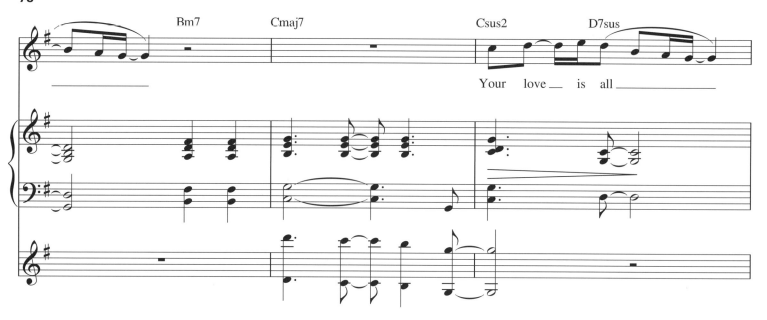

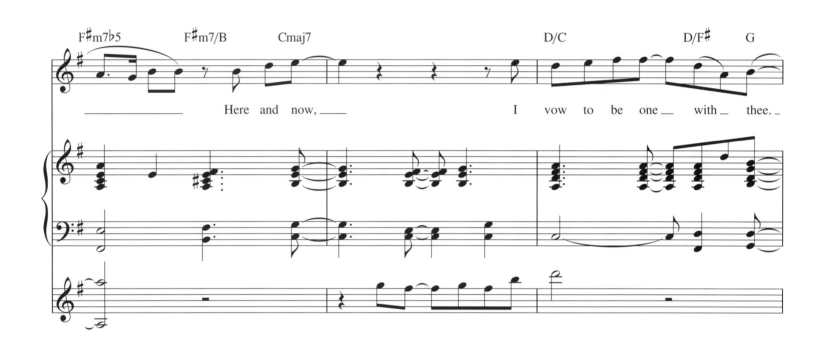
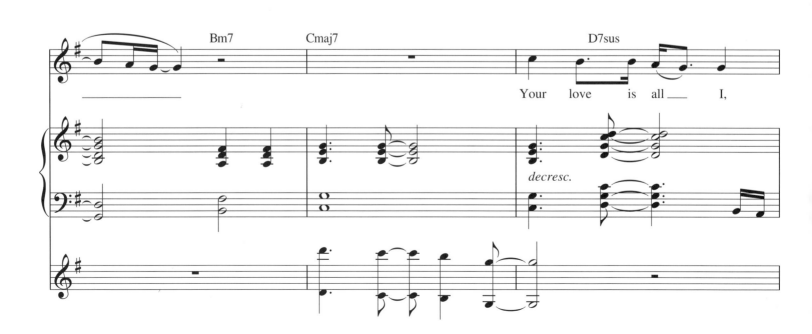

Higher Ground

Words and Music by
Stevie Wonder

Moderately fast ($\. = 126$)

* Multiple parts have been combined to be playable by two keyboards.

© 1973 (Renewed 2001) JOBETE MUSIC CO., INC. and BLACK BULL MUSIC
c/o EMI APRIL MUSIC INC.
All Rights Reserved   International Copyright Secured   Used by Permission

* *Vocal sung as written.*

88

90

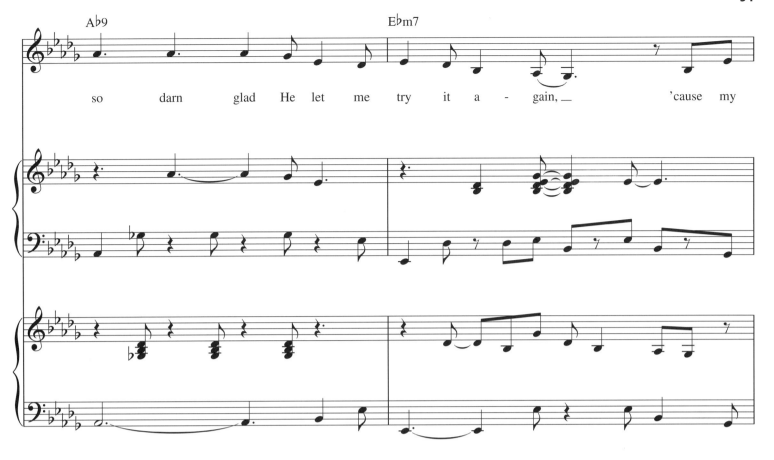

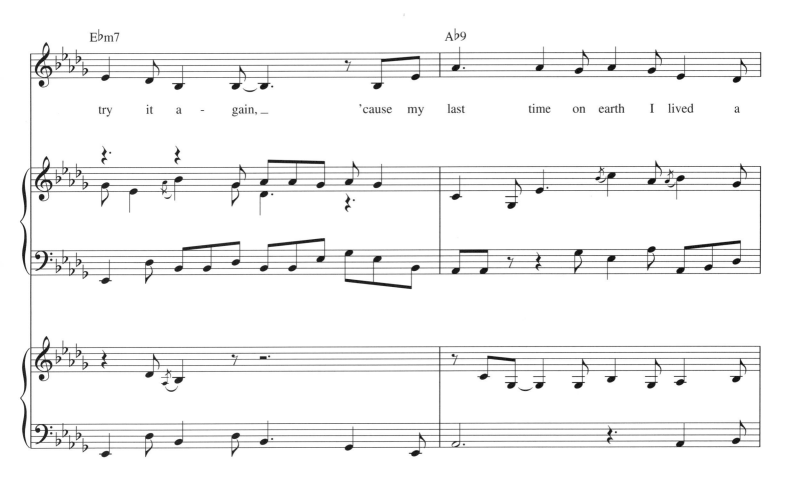

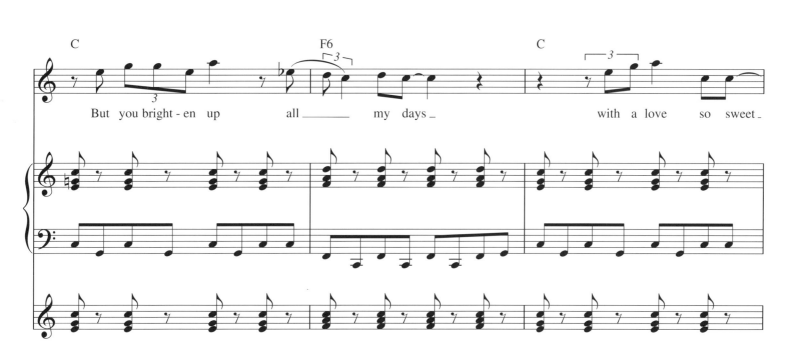

Background vocals sung as written.

I Can't Get Next to You

Words and Music by Barrett Strong
and Norman Whitfield

I Can't Help Myself
(Sugar Pie, Honey Bunch)

Words and Music by Brian Holland,
Lamont Dozier and Edward Holland

Moderately fast (♩ = 130)

© 1965, 1972 (Renewed 1993, 2000) JOBETE MUSIC CO., INC.
All Rights Controlled and Administered by EMI BLACKWOOD MUSIC INC. on behalf of STONE AGATE MUSIC (A Division of JOBETE MUSIC CO., INC.)
All Rights Reserved   International Copyright Secured   Used by Permission

125

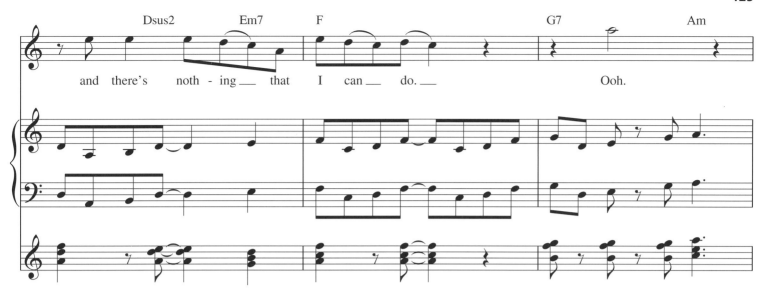

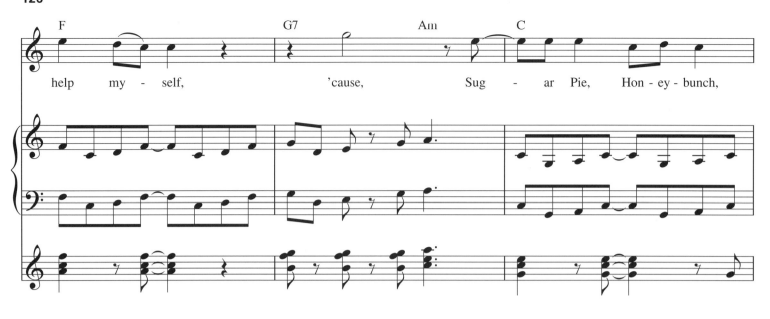

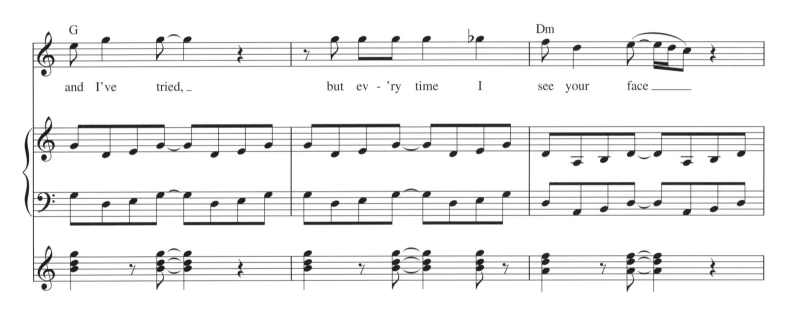

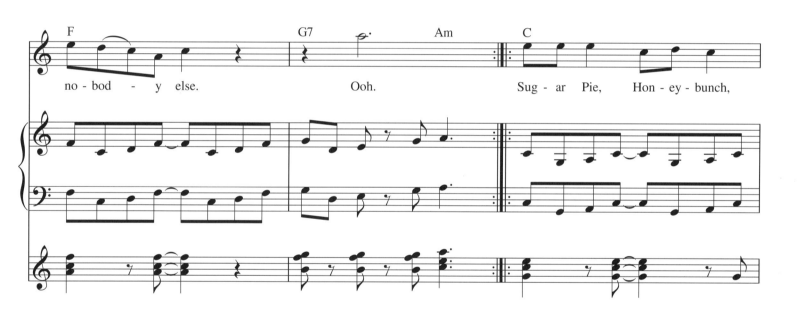

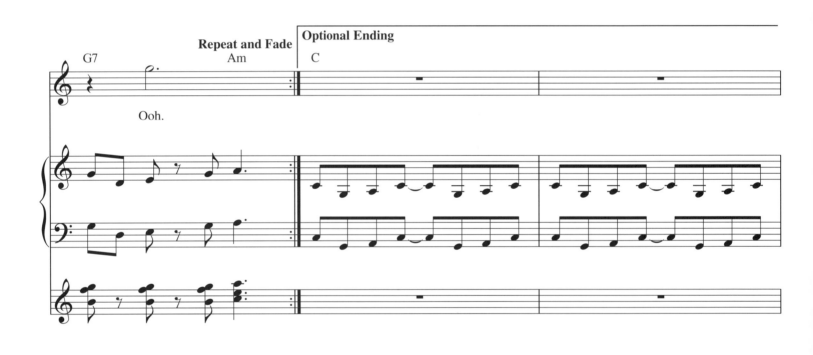

I Heard It Through the Grapevine

Words and Music by Norman J. Whitfield
and Barrett Strong

* Vocals sung as written.

© 1966 (Renewed 1994) JOBETE MUSIC CO., INC.
All Rights Controlled and Administered by EMI BLACKWOOD MUSIC INC. on behalf of STONE AGATE MUSIC (A Division of JOBETE MUSIC CO., INC.)
All Rights Reserved   International Copyright Secured   Used by Permission

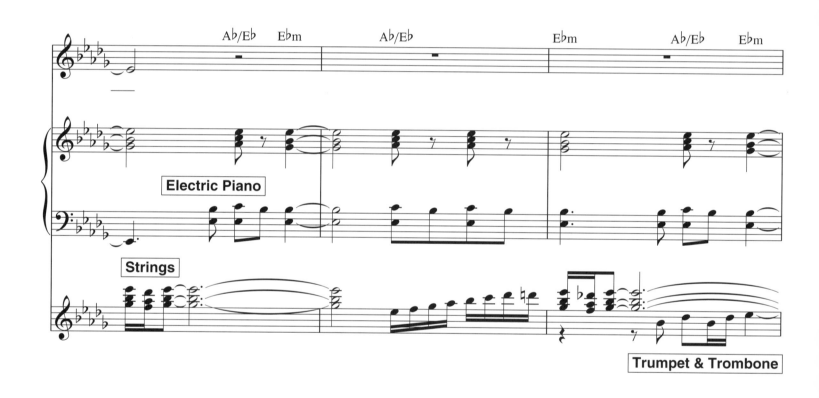

I Wish

Words and Music by Stevie Wonder

* In order to avoid overlap with the R.H., much of the
  L.H. has been written an octave lower than recorded.

© 1976 JOBETE MUSIC CO., INC. and BLACK BULL MUSIC
c/o EMI APRIL MUSIC INC.
All Rights Reserved   International Copyright Secured   Used by Permission

*Vocals sung as written.

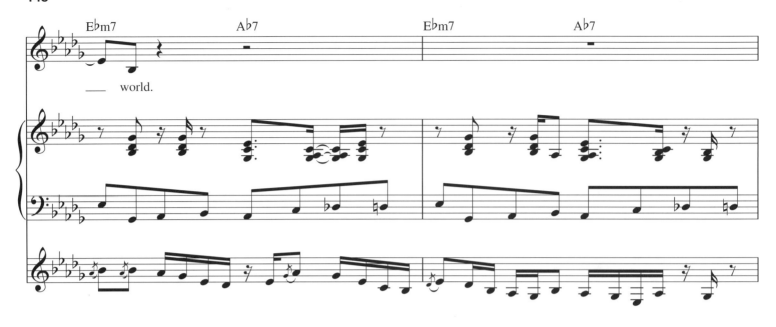

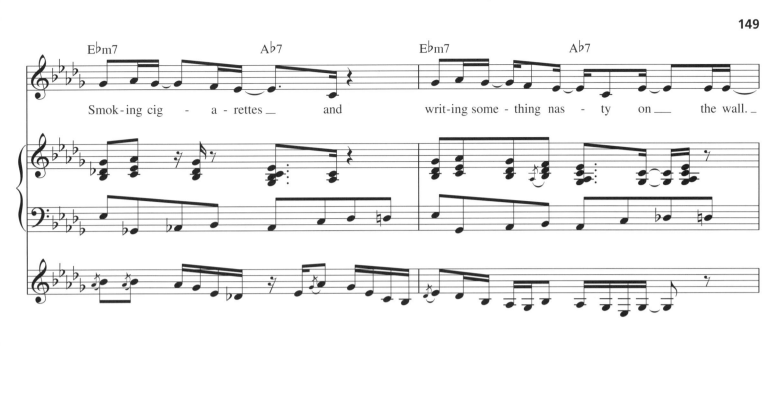

150

You grow up and learn that kind-a thing ain't right,

but while you were do-ing it, it sure felt out-ta sight. I wish those

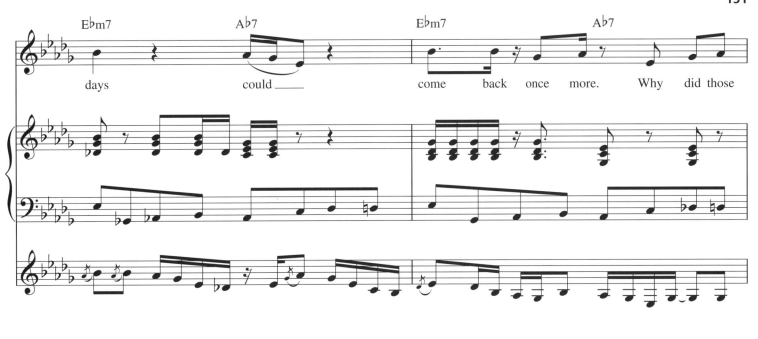

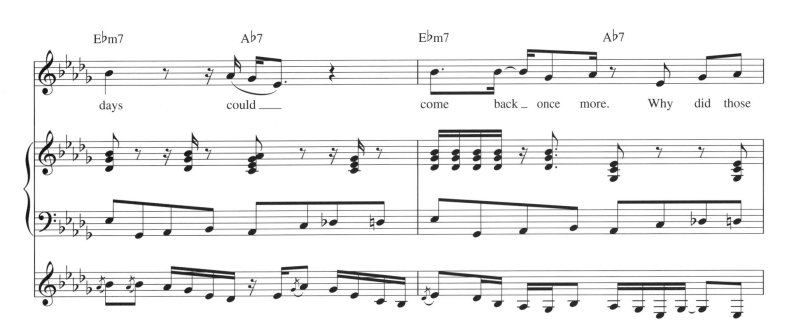

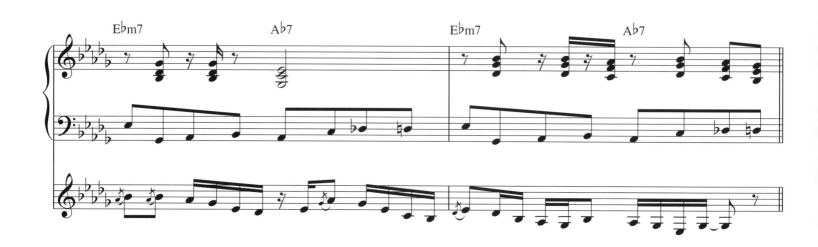

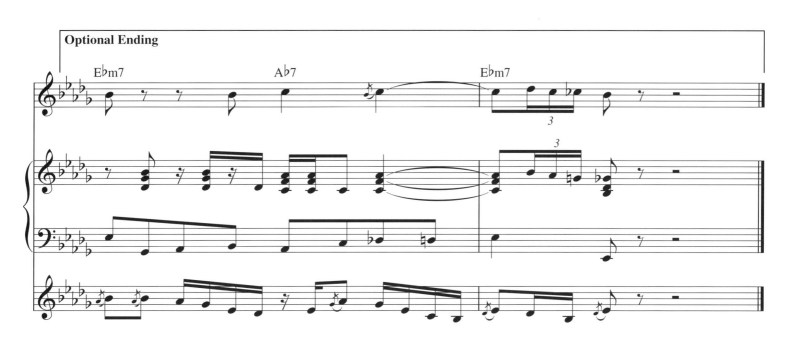

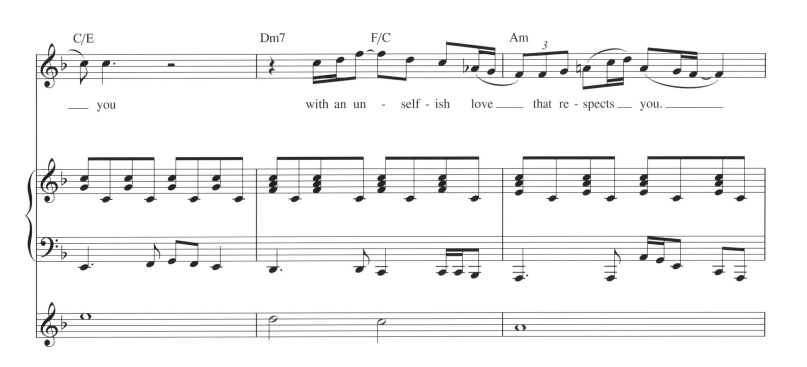

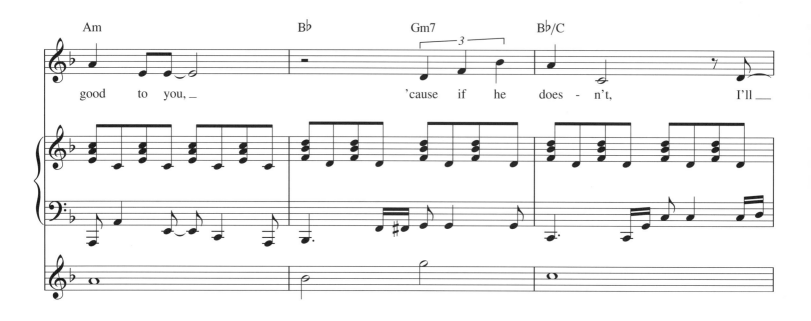

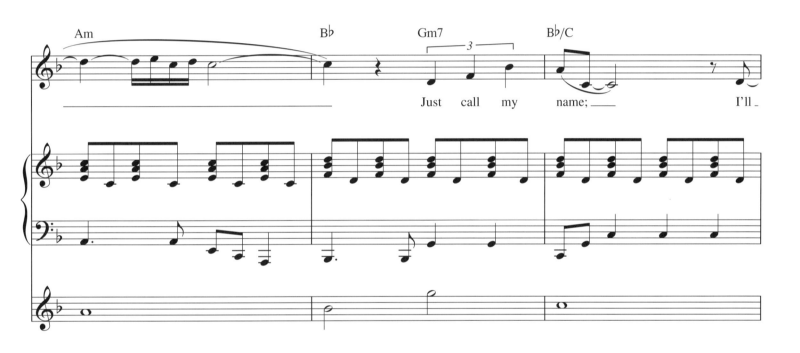
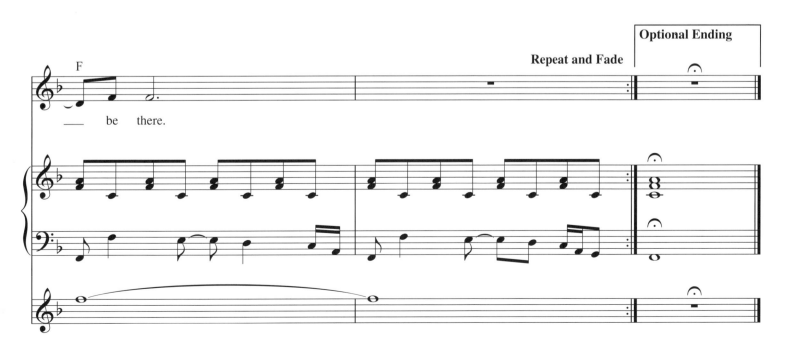

Just Once

Words by Cynthia Weil
Music by Barry Mann

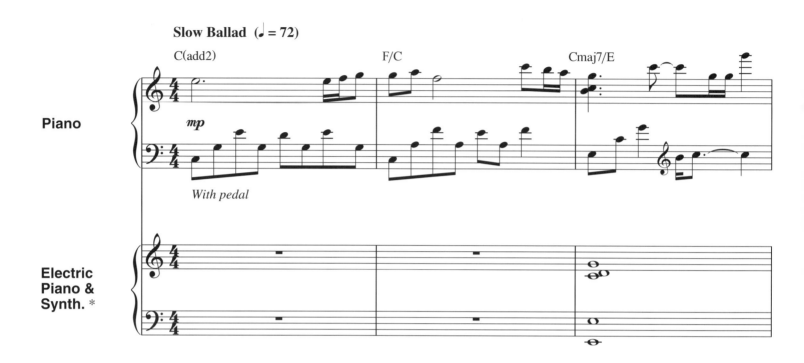

*Multiple parts have been combined to be playable by one keyboard.

Copyright © 1981 Sony/ATV Songs LLC and Mann & Weil Songs, Inc.
All Rights Administered by Sony/ATV Music Publishing, 8 Music Square West, Nashville, TN 37203
International Copyright Secured   All Rights Reserved

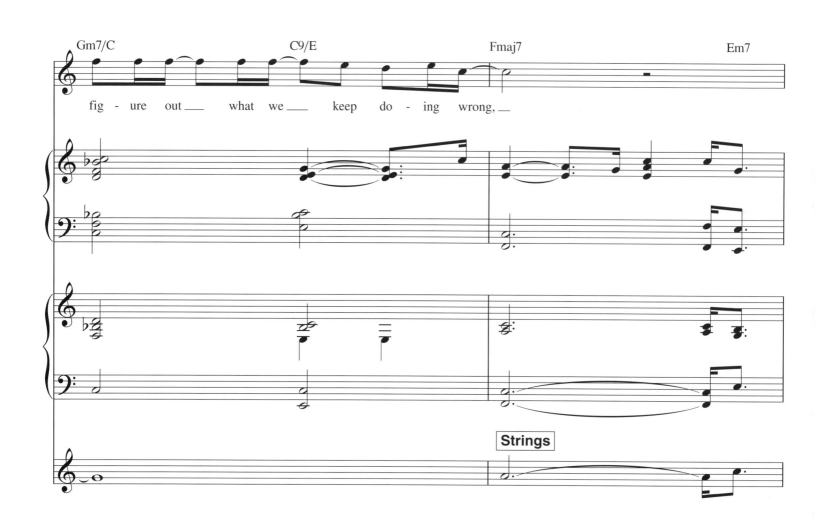

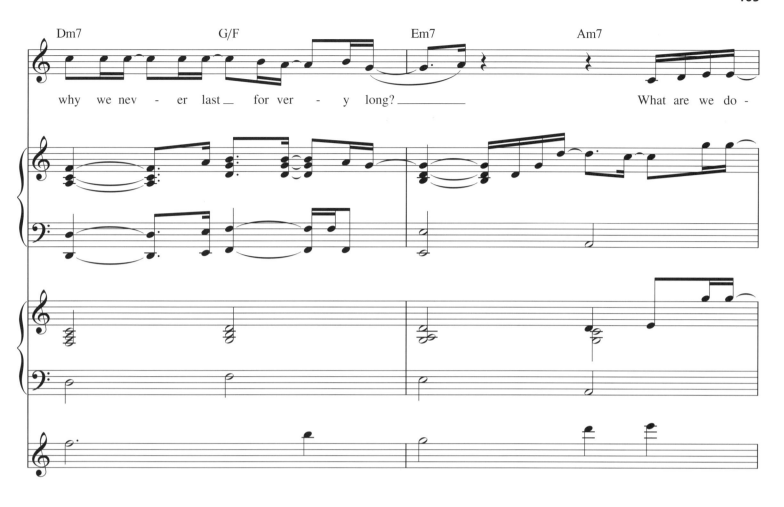
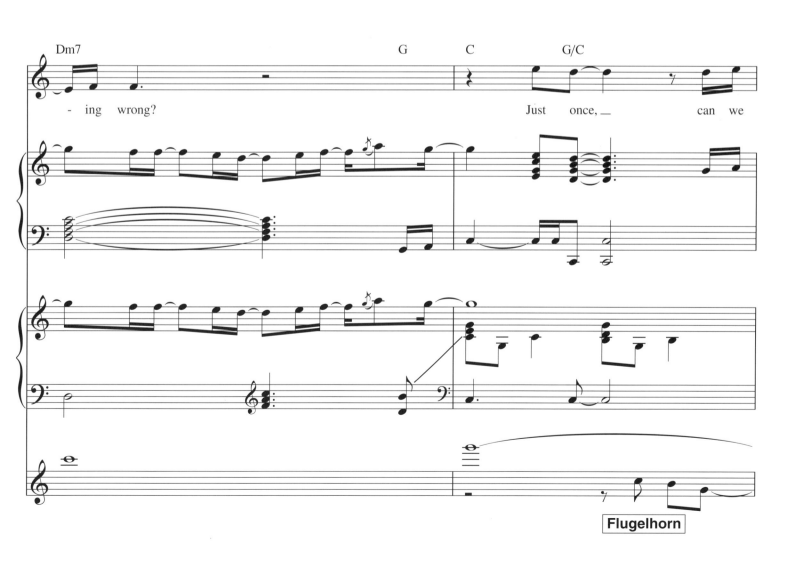

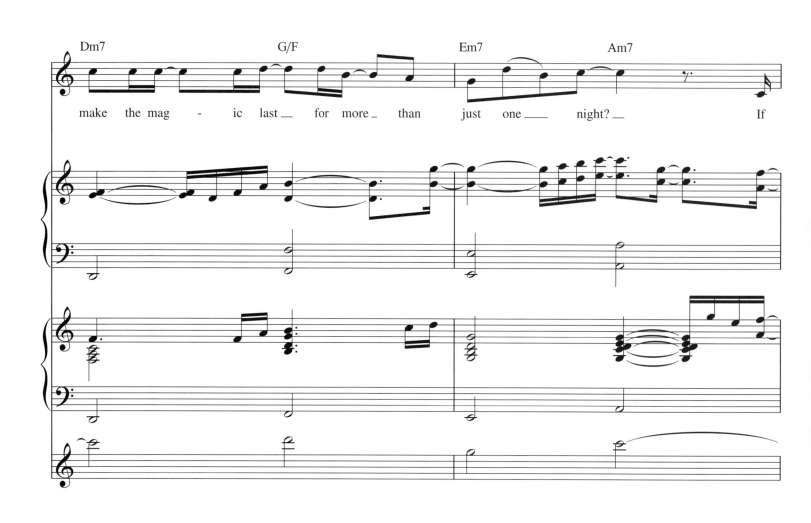

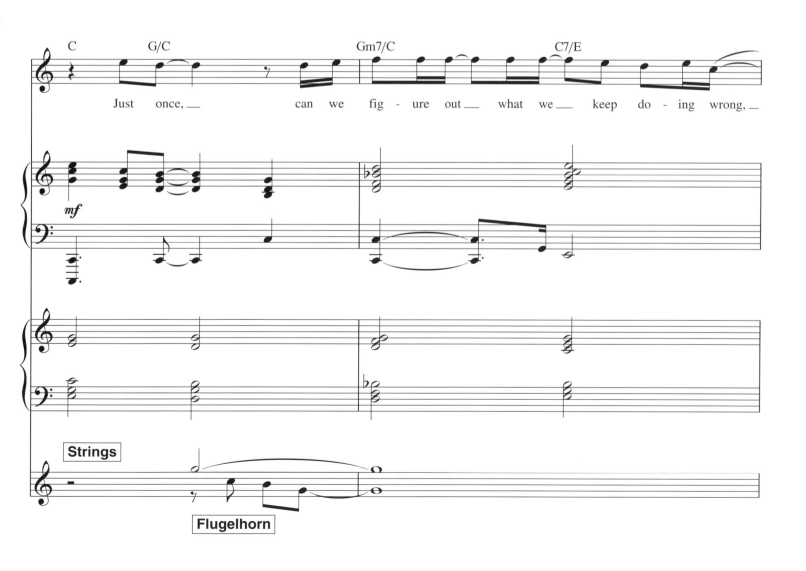

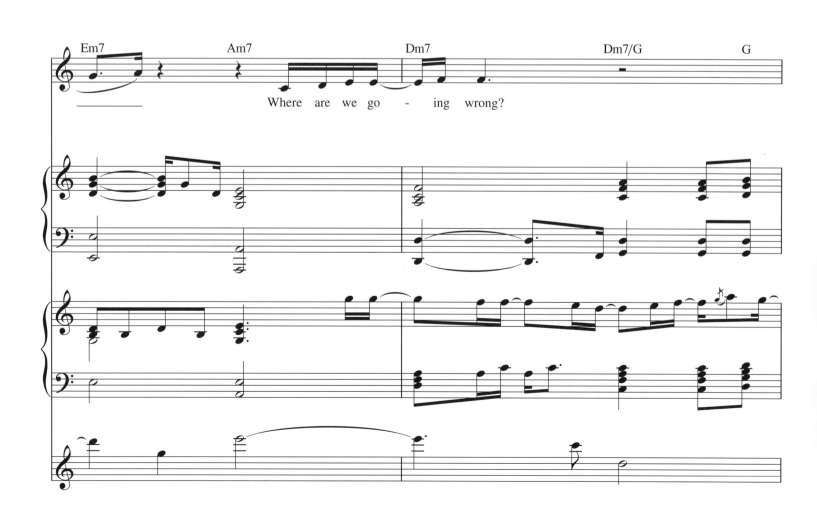

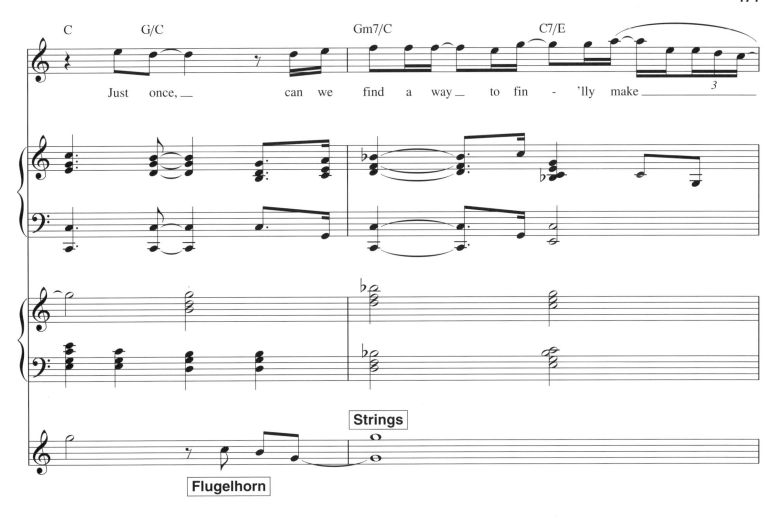
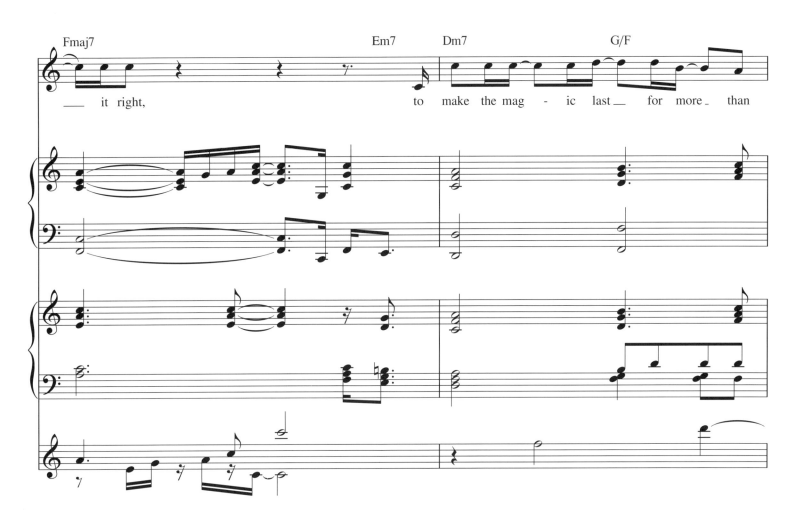

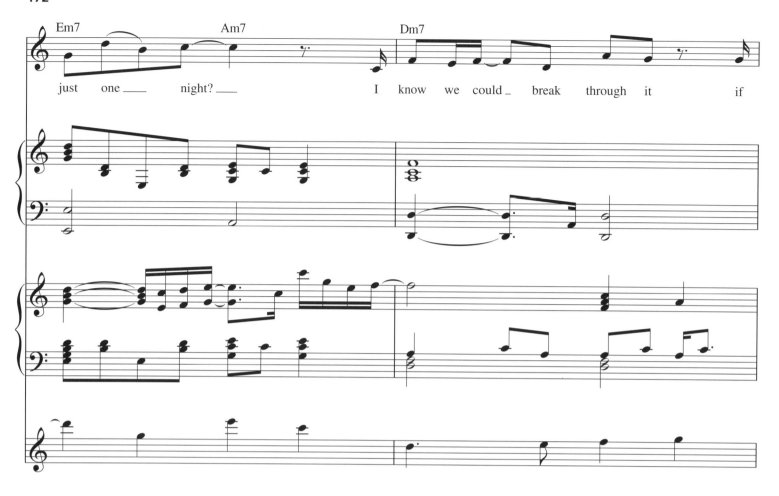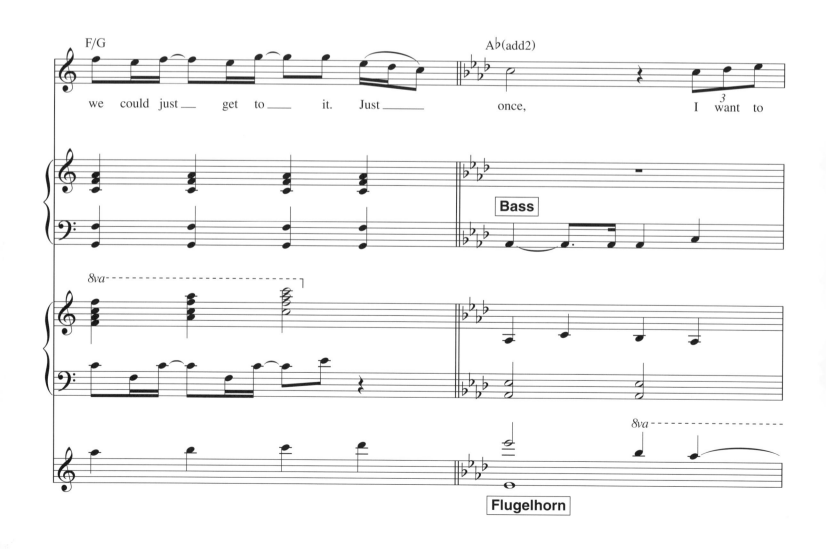

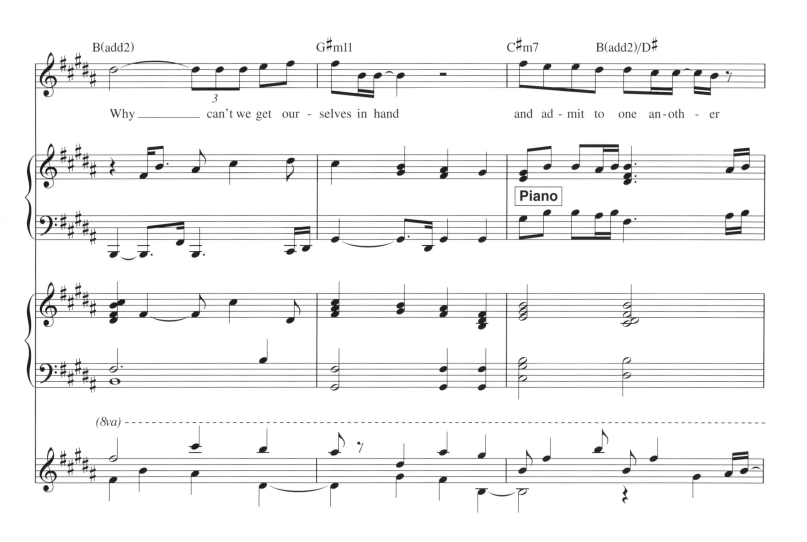

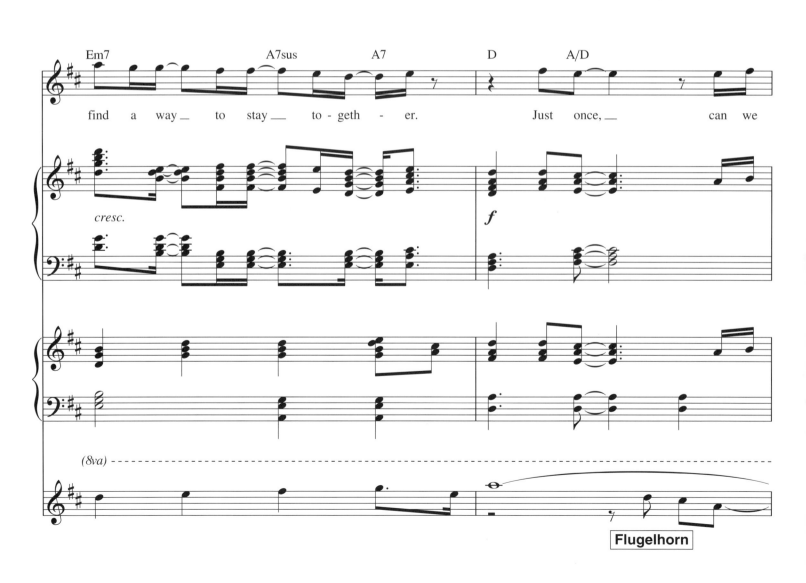

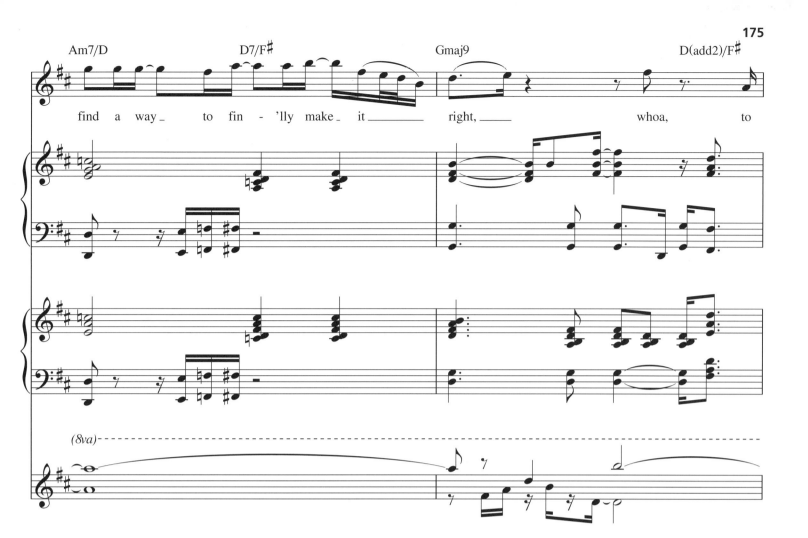

Lady Marmalade

Words and Music by Bob Crewe
and Kenny Nolan

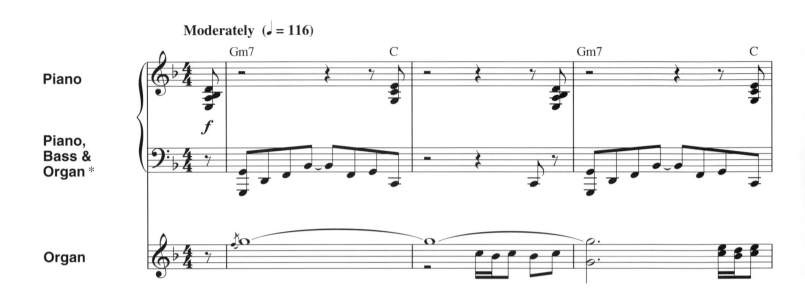

*Multiple parts have been combined to be playable by one keyboard.

© 1974 JOBETE MUSIC CO., INC., STONE DIAMOND MUSIC CORP., TANNYBOY MUSIC CO. and KENNY NOLAN PUBLISHING
All Rights Controlled and Administered by EMI APRIL MUSIC INC. and EMI BLACKWOOD MUSIC INC.
All Rights Reserved   International Copyright Secured   Used by Permission

184

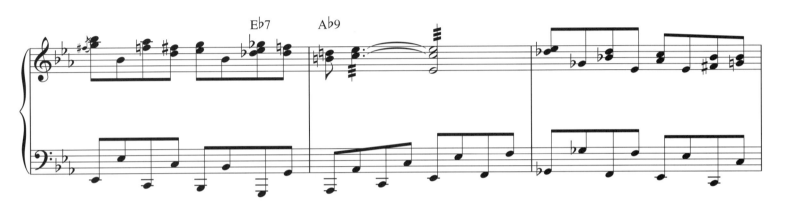

196

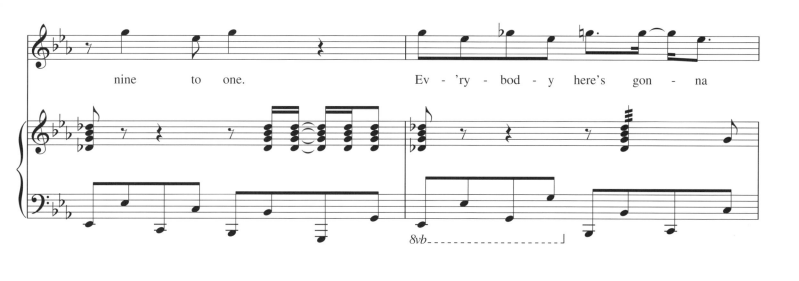

Miss You Like Crazy

Words and Music by Gerry Goffin,
Preston Glass and Michael Masser

* Multiple parts have been combined to be playable by one keyboard.

© 1989 SCREEN GEMS-EMI MUSIC INC., LAUREN-WESLEY MUSIC, IRVING MUSIC INC., GEMIA MUSIC and PRINCE STREET MUSIC
All Rights for LAUREN-WESLEY MUSIC Controlled and Administered by SCREEN GEMS-EMI MUSIC INC.
All Rights Reserved   International Copyright Secured   Used by Permission

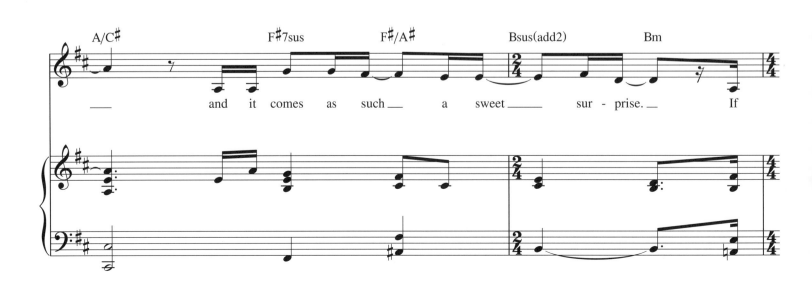

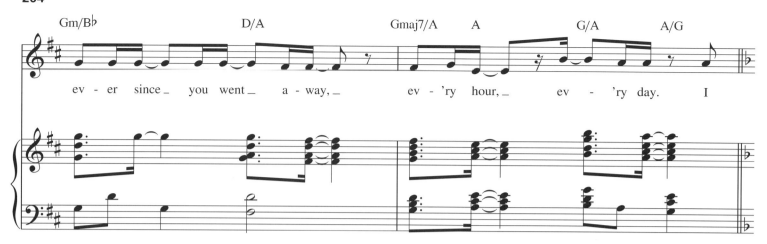

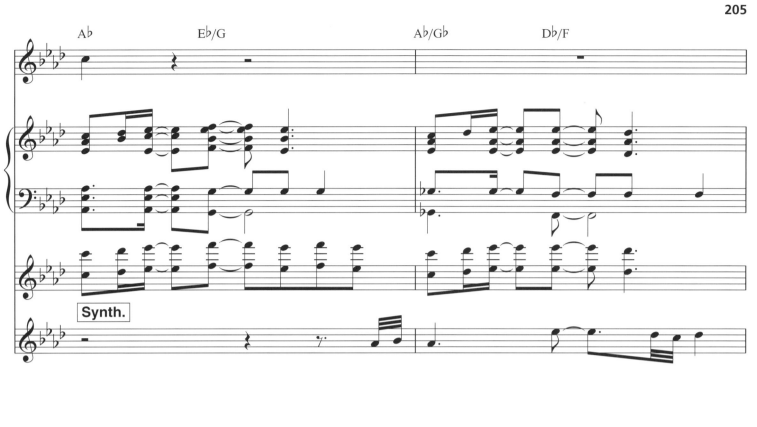
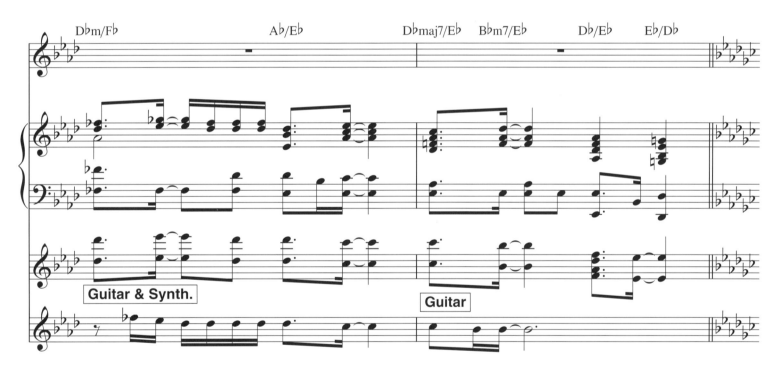

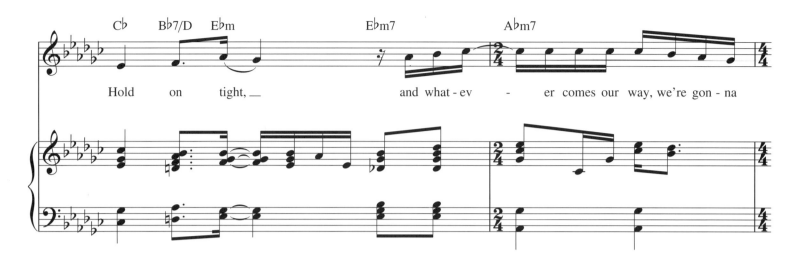
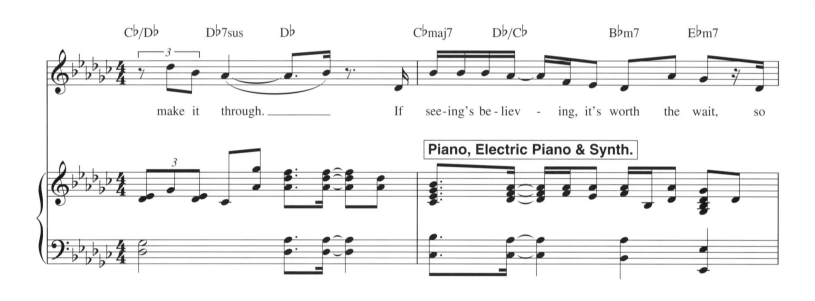

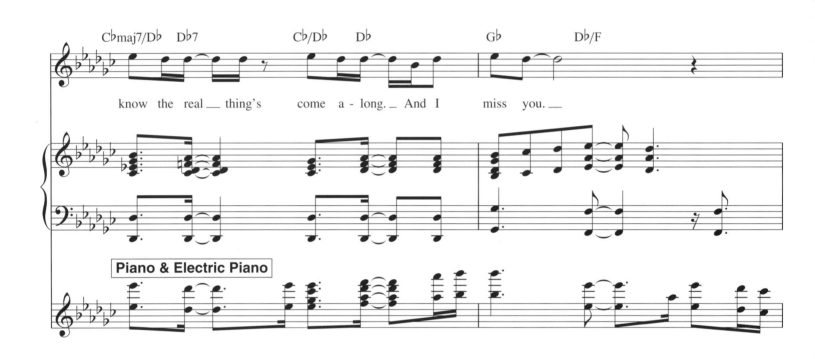

Money
(That's What I Want)

Words and Music by Berry Gordy and Janie Bradford

* Omit "uh-huh" last time.

Nothing from Nothing

Words and Music by Billy Preston
and Bruce Fisher

* Two Piano parts have been combined to be playable by one piano.

Copyright © 1974 ALMO MUSIC CORP. and IRVING MUSIC, INC.
All Rights Reserved Used by Permission

218

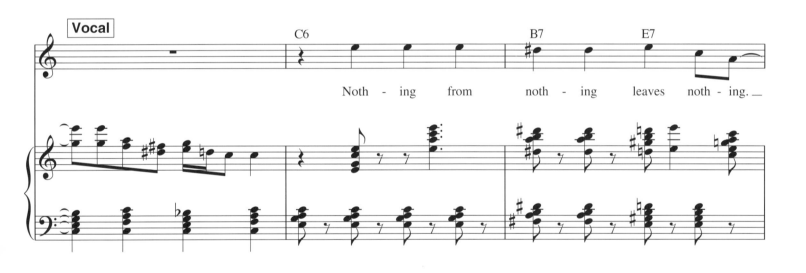

Nothing from nothing leaves nothing.

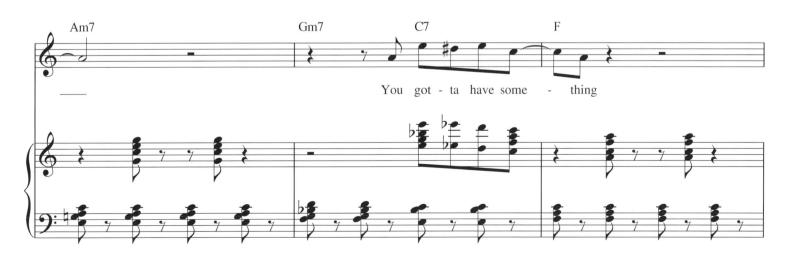

You gotta have something

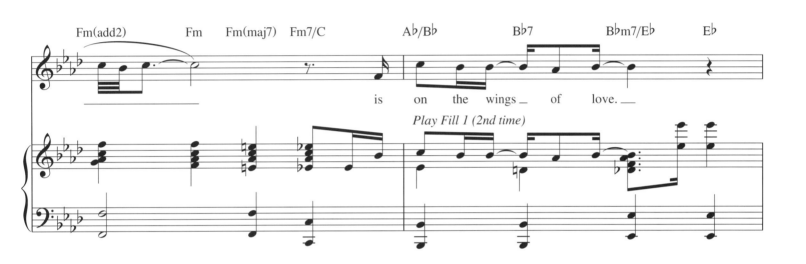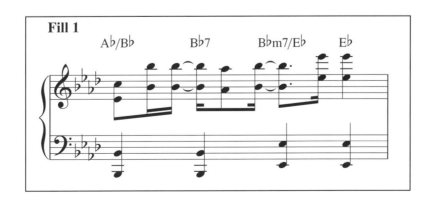

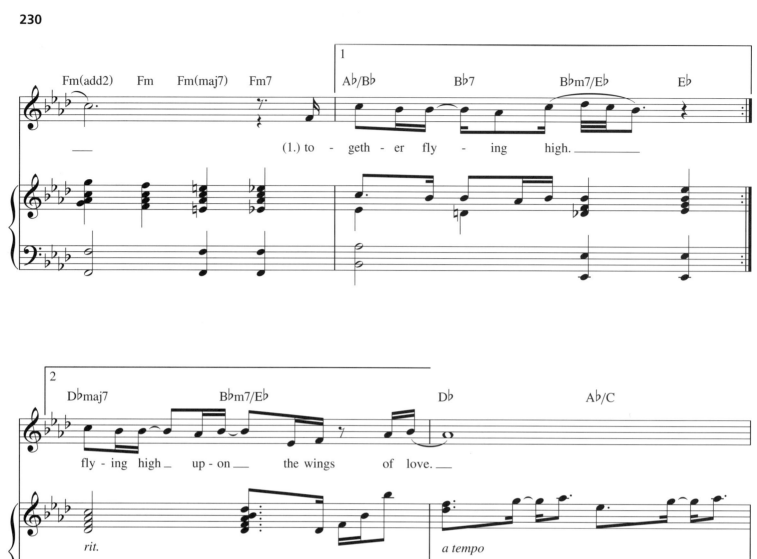

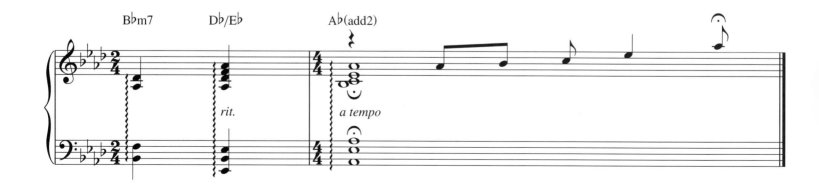

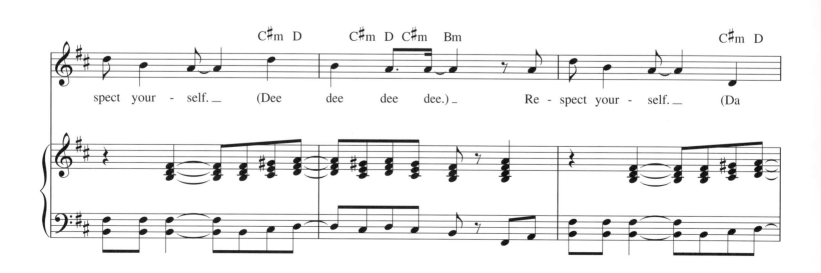

Ribbon in the Sky

Words and Music by
Stevie Wonder

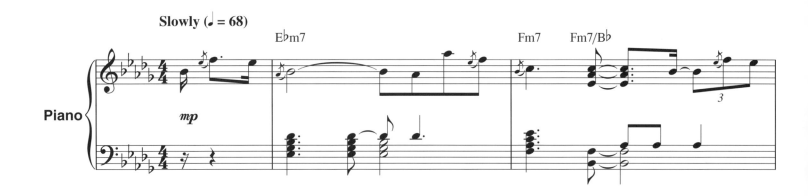

© 1982 JOBETE MUSIC CO., INC. and BLACK BULL MUSIC
c/o EMI APRIL MUSIC INC.
All Rights Reserved   International Copyright Secured   Used by Permission

Sail On

Words and Music by
Lionel Richie

249

© 1979 JOBETE MUSIC CO., INC. and LIBREN MUSIC
All Rights Controlled and Administered by EMI APRIL MUSIC INC.
All Rights Reserved   International Copyright Secured   Used by Permission

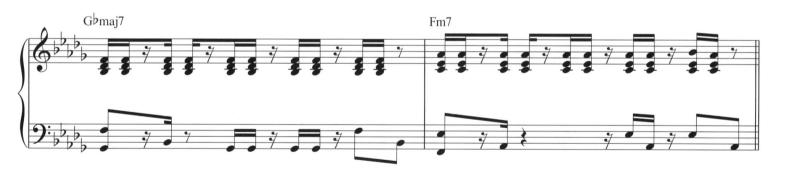

Send One Your Love

Words and Music by
Stevie Wonder

* Multiple parts have been combined to be playable by one keyboard.

© 1979 JOBETE MUSIC CO., INC. and BLACK BULL MUSIC
c/o EMI APRIL MUSIC INC.
All Rights Reserved   International Copyright Secured   Used by Permission

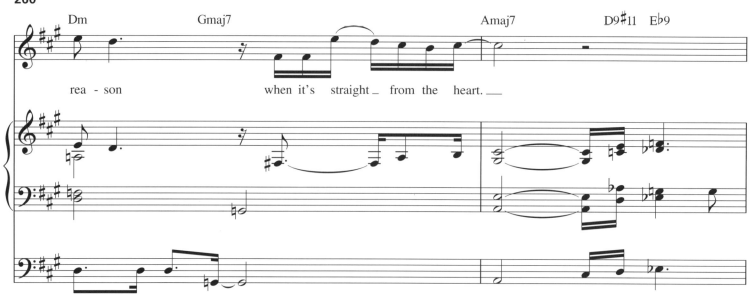
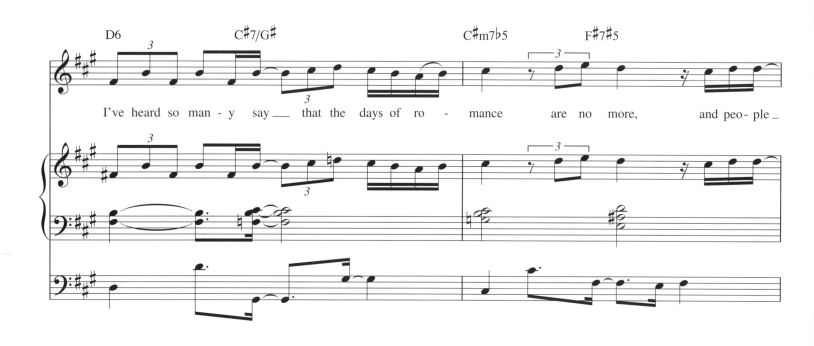

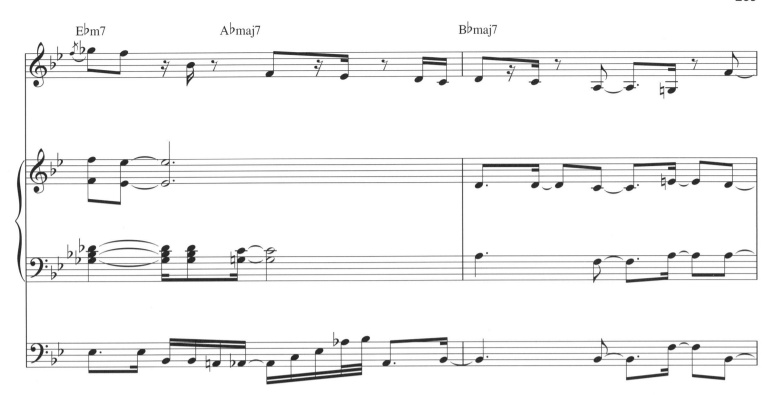

Superstition

Words and Music by
Stevie Wonder

Moderately (♩ = 104)

© 1972 (Renewed 2000) JOBETE MUSIC CO., INC. and BLACK BULL MUSIC
c/o EMI APRIL MUSIC INC.
All Rights Reserved   International Copyright Secured   Used by Permission

273

274

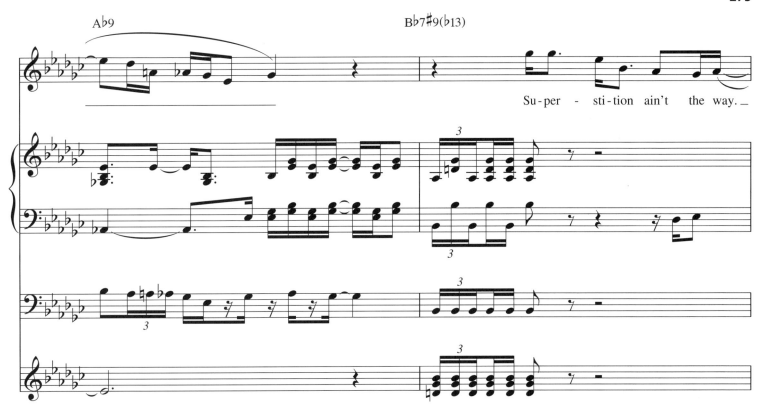

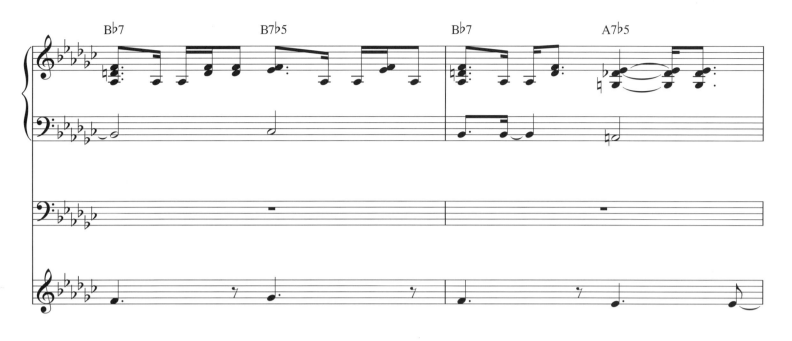
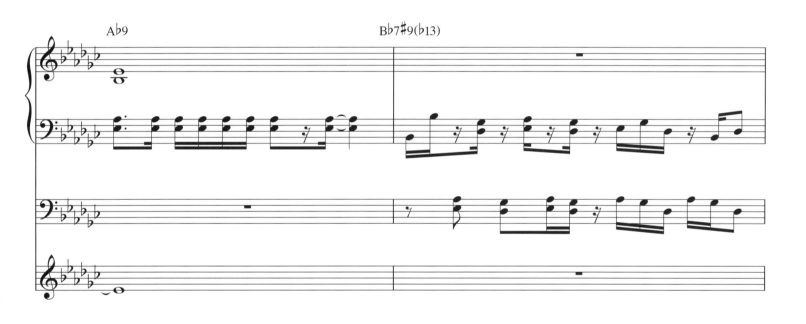

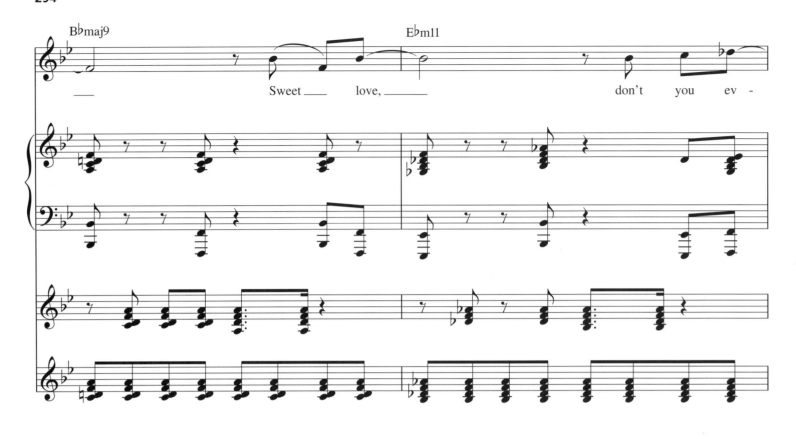

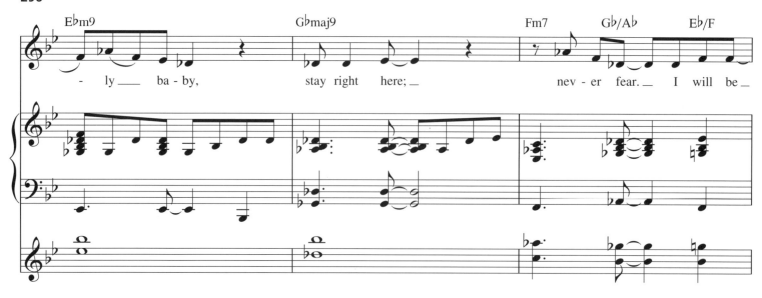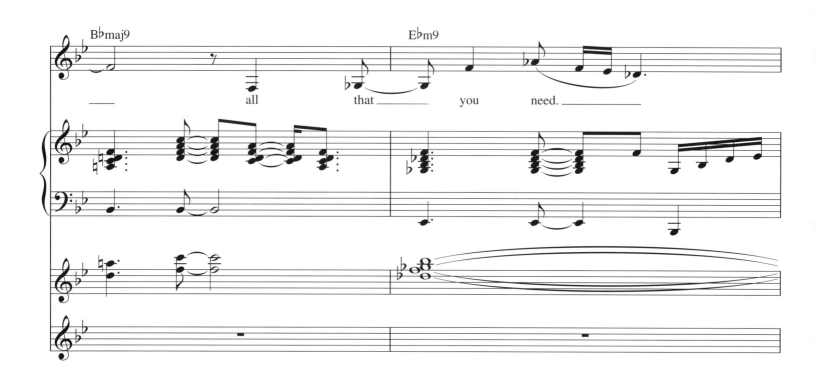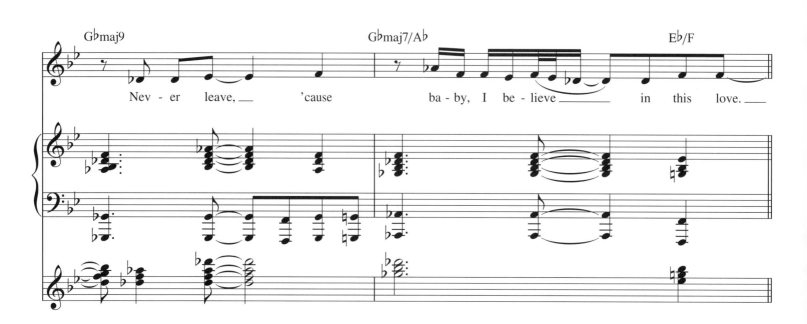

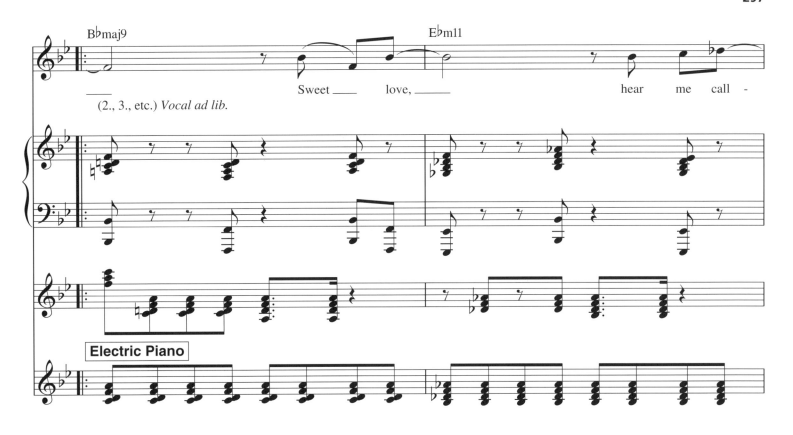
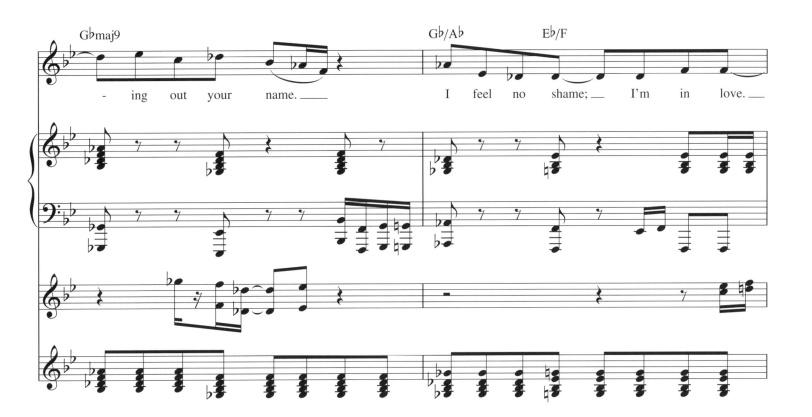

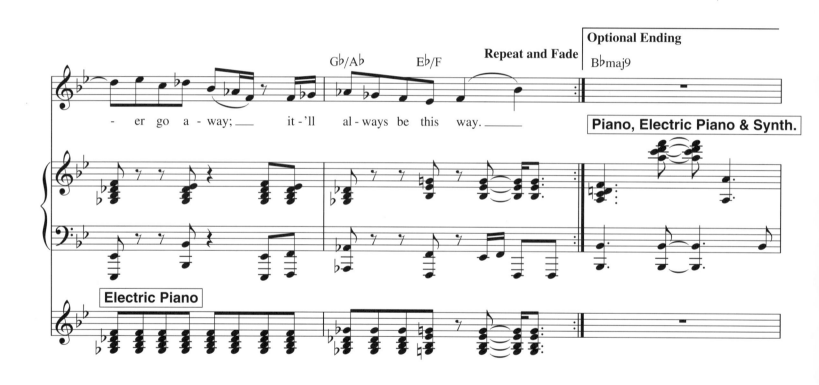
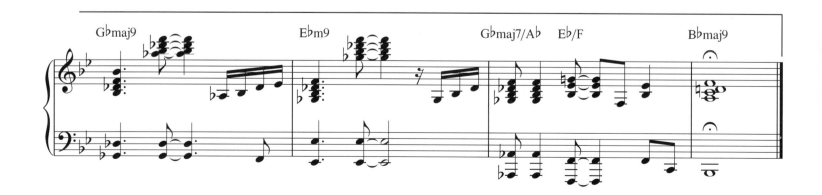

This Masquerade

Words and Music by
Leon Russell

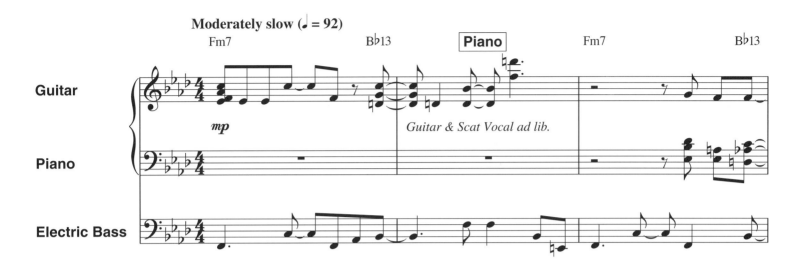
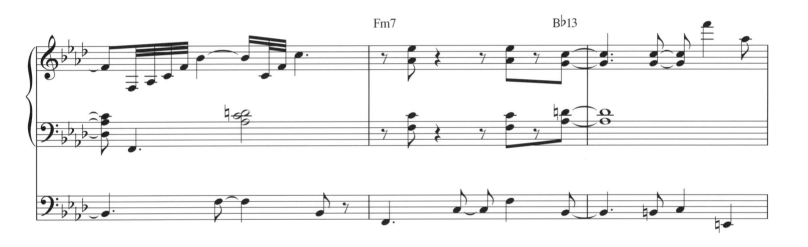

Copyright © 1972, 1973; Renewed 2000, 2001 DreamWorks Music Publishing LLC d/b/a Stuck On Music (BMI) and Embassy Music Corp. (BMI)
Worldwide Rights for DreamWorks Music Publishing LLC d/b/a Stuck On Music Administered by Cherry River Music Co.
International Copyright Secured   All Rights Reserved

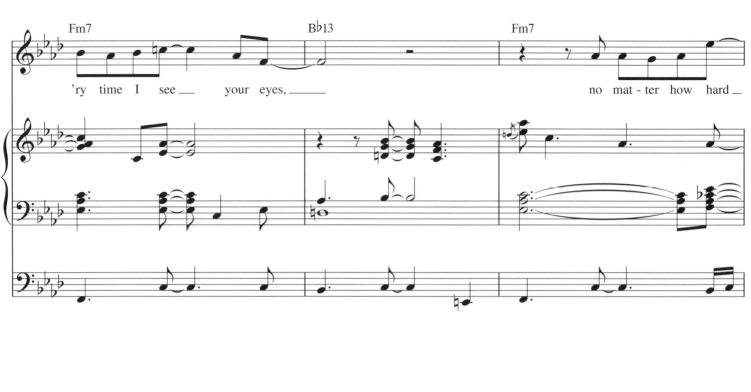

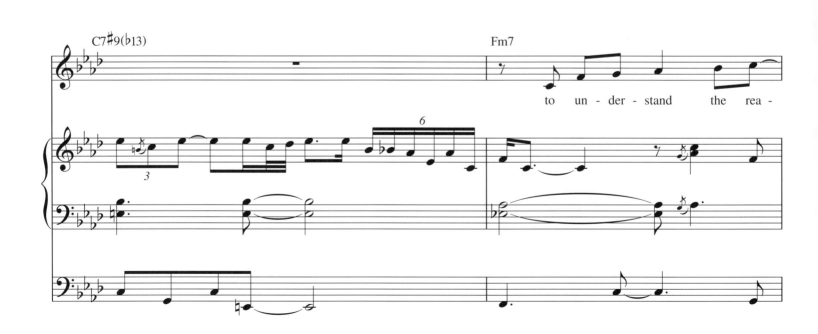

Tell It Like It Is

Words and Music by George Davis
and Lee Diamond

Slowly, steadily (♩. = 64)

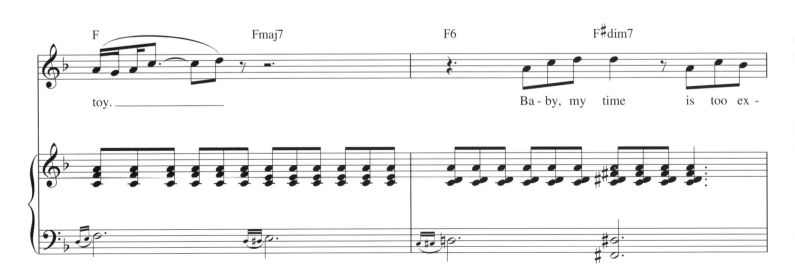

Copyright © 1966 (Renewed), 1980 by Olrap Publishing Co., Inc. (BMI) and Conrad Music, a division of Arc Music Corp. (BMI)
International Copyright Secured   All Rights Reserved
Used by Permission

Three Times a Lady

Words and Music by
Lionel Richie

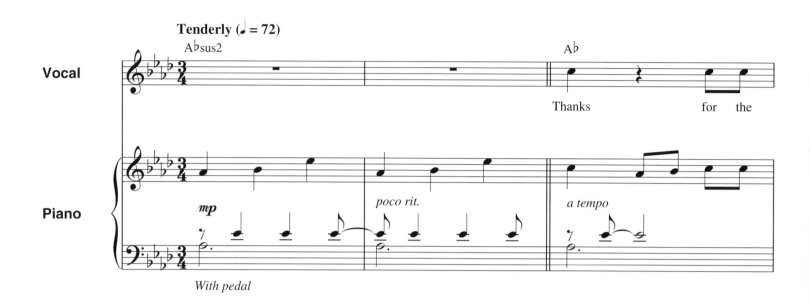

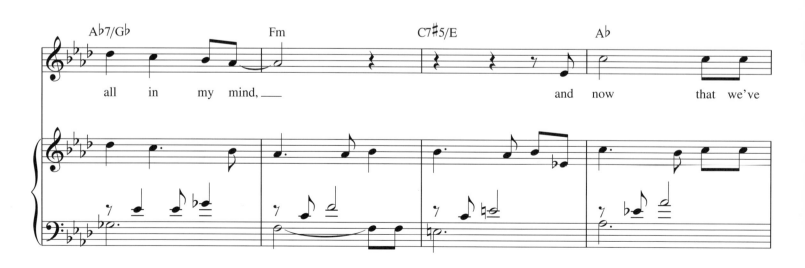

© 1978 JOBETE MUSIC CO., INC. and LIBREN MUSIC
All Rights Controlled and Administered by EMI APRIL MUSIC INC.
All Rights Reserved   International Copyright Secured   Used by Permission

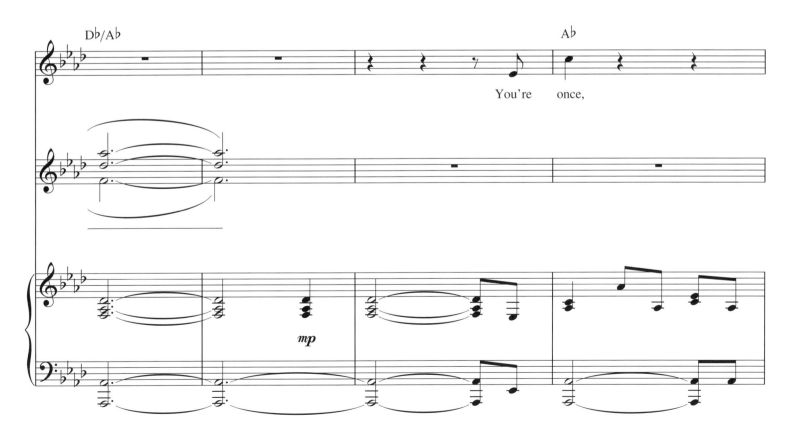

twice, three times a la-dy, and I love you, I love you.

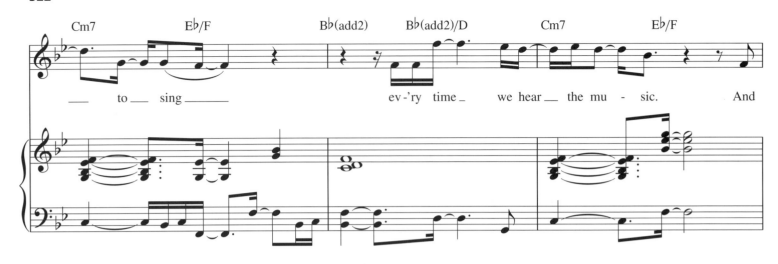
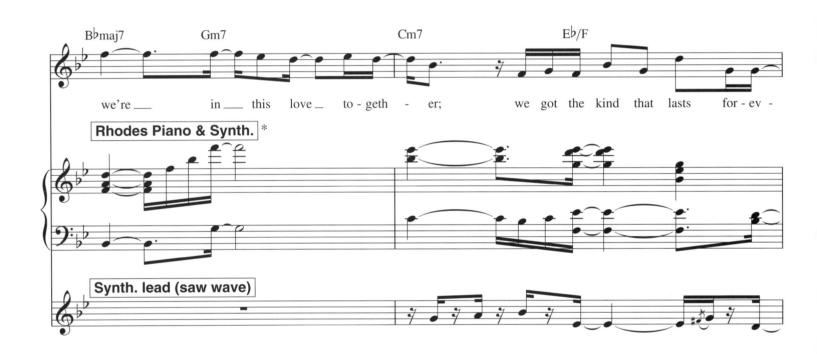
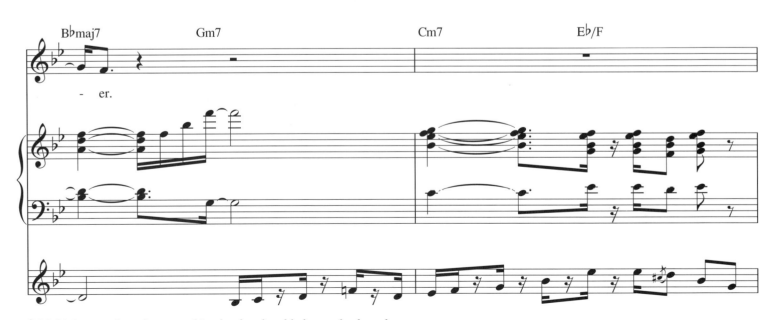

*Multiple parts have been combined to be playable by one keyboard.

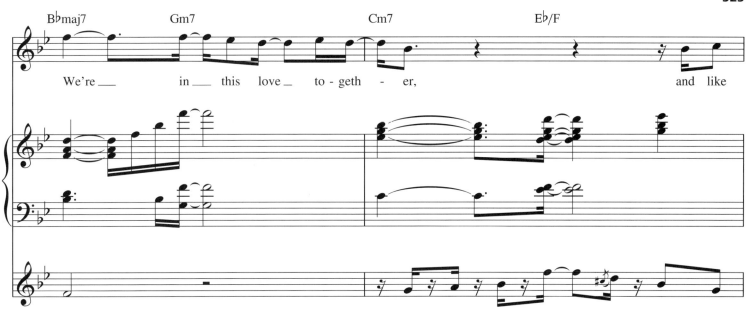

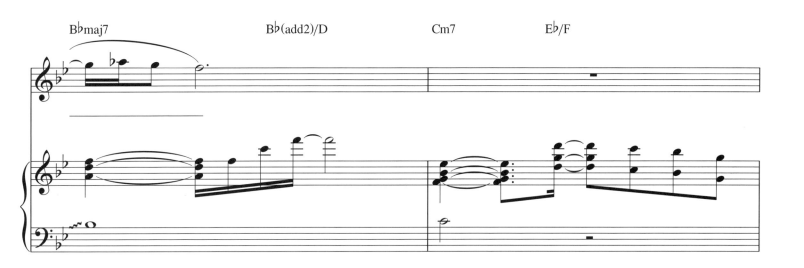

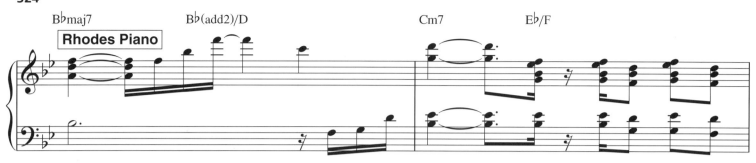
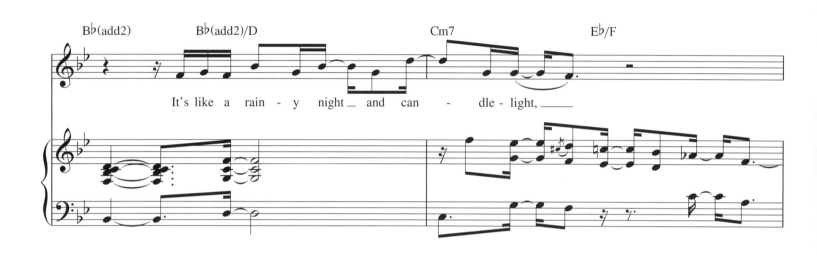

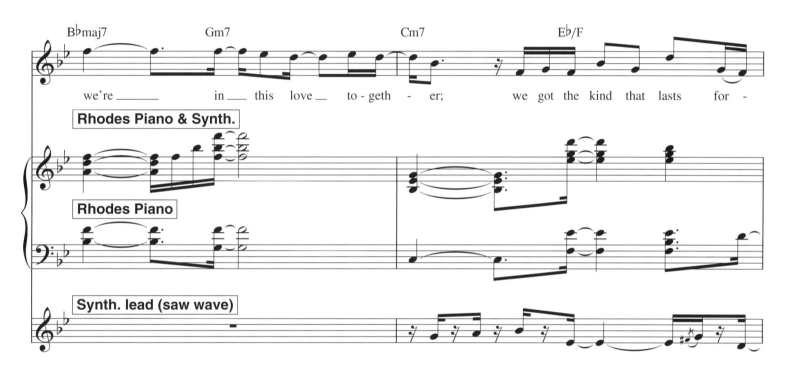
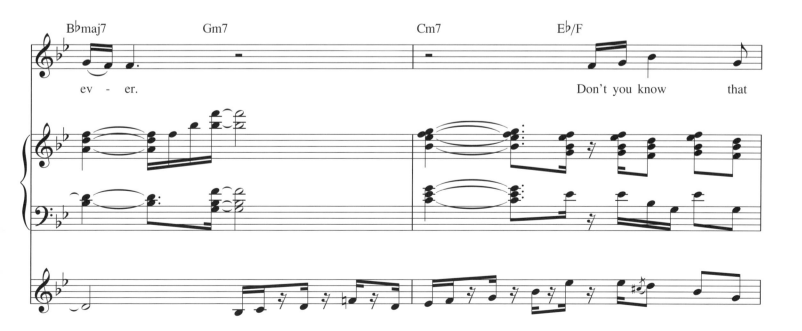

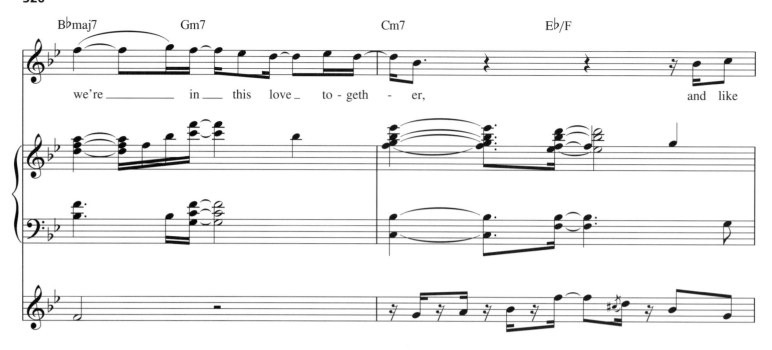

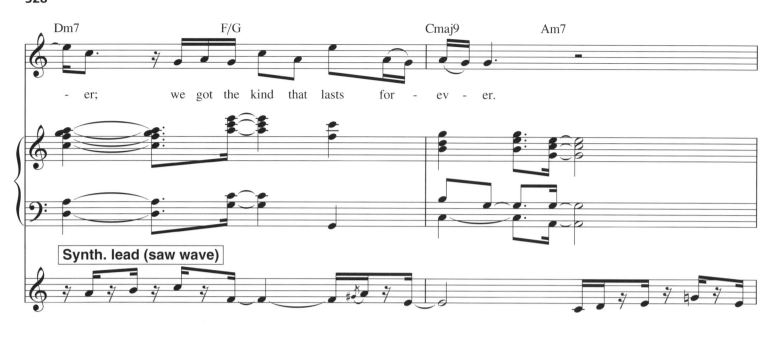
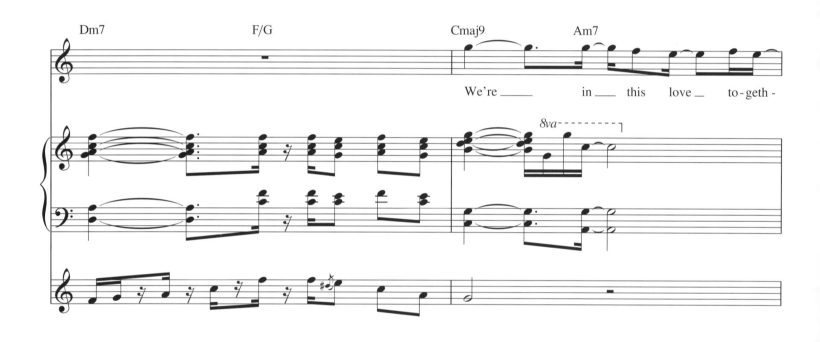

What'd I Say?

Words and Music by
Ray Charles

Copyright © 1959 by Unichappell Music Inc.
Copyright Renewed
International Copyright Secured   All Rights Reserved

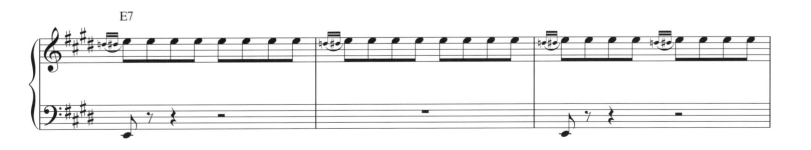

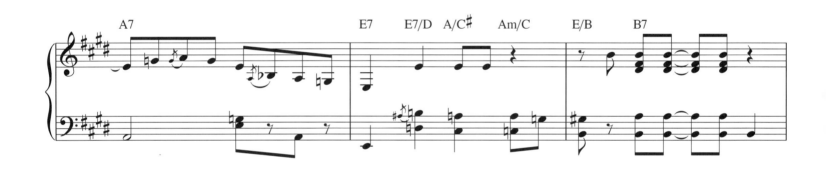

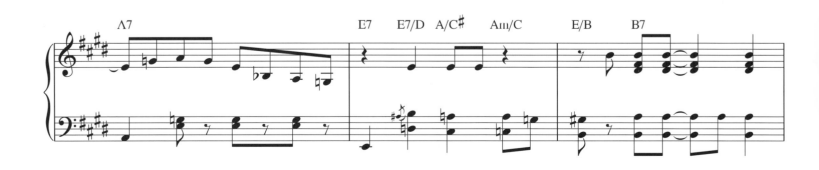

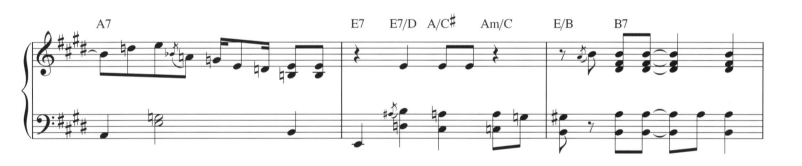
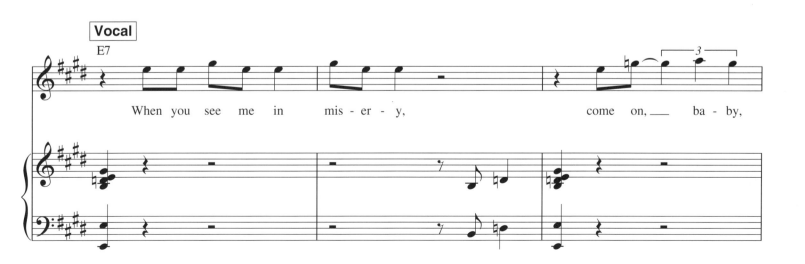

Additional Lyrics

2. Oh, make me feel so good. (Make me feel so good.)
   Make me feel so good now, yeah. (Make me feel so good.)
   Oh, baby. (Make me feel so good.)
   Make me feel so good, yeah. (Make me feel so good.)
   Make me feel so good. (Make me feel so good.)
   Make me feel so good, yeah. (Make me feel so good.)

3. Oh, it's all right. (Baby, it's all right.)
   Said a-it's all right, right now. (Baby, it's all right.)
   Said a-it's all right. (Baby, it's all right.)
   Said a-it's all right, yeah. (Baby, it's all right.)
   Said a-it's all right. (Baby, it's all right.)
   Said a-it's all right. (Baby, it's all right.)

NOTE-FOR-NOTE KEYBOARD TRANSCRIPTIONS

These outstanding collections feature note-for-note transcriptions from the artists who made the songs famous. No matter what style you play, these books are perfect for performers or students who want to play just like their keyboard idols.

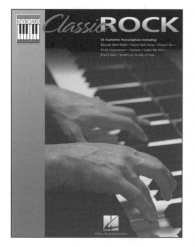

CLASSIC ROCK

Authentic transcriptions – right off the recordings! – of these 35 all-time rock classics: Beth • Bloody Well Right • Changes • Cold as Ice • Come Sail Away • Don't Do Me Like That • Green-Eyed Lady • Hard to Handle • Heaven • Killer Queen • King of Pain • Lady Madonna • Layla • Light My Fire • Oye Como Va • Piano Man • Takin' Care of Business • Werewolves of London • Woman from Tokyo • and more.

00310940 Keyboard Transcriptions.................................$24.95

POP/ROCK

35 note-for-note transcriptions for those who want to play *exactly* what they hear on recordings. Songs include: Africa • Against All Odds • Axel F • Centerfold • Chariots of Fire • Cherish • Don't Let the Sun Go Down on Me • Drops of Jupiter (Tell Me) • Faithfully • It's Too Late • Just the Way You Are • Let It Be • Mandy • Sailing • Sweet Dreams Are Made of This • Walking in Memphis.

00310939 Keyboard Transcriptions.................................$24.95

JAZZ

Authentic note-for-note transcriptions of 24 favorites from jazz piano masters including Bill Evans, Thelonious Monk, Oscar Peterson, Bud Powell, and Art Tatum. Includes: Ain't Misbehavin' • April in Paris • Autumn in New York • Body and Soul • Freddie Freeloader • Giant Steps • My Foolish Heart • My Funny Valentine • Satin Doll • Song for My Father • Stella by Starlight • and more.

00310941 Keyboard Transcriptions.................................$22.95

R&B

Exact transcriptions straight from the recordings of 35 R&B classics: Baby Love • Boogie on Reggae Woman • Easy • Endless Love • Fallin' • Green Onions • Higher Ground • I'll Be There • Just Once • Money (That's What I Want) • On the Wings of Love • Ribbon in the Sky • This Masquerade • Three Times a Lady.

00310942 Keyboard Transcriptions.................................$24.95

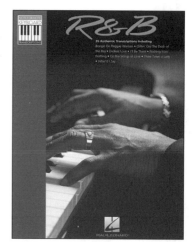

THE CAROLE KING KEYBOARD BOOK

Note-for-note transcriptions of all the piano and keyboard parts on 16 of King's greatest songs: Beautiful • Been to Canaan • Home Again • I Feel the Earth Move • It's Too Late • Jazzman • (You Make Me Feel) Like a Natural Woman • Nightingale • Smackwater Jack • So Far Away • Sweet Seasons • Tapestry • Way Over Yonder • Where You Lead • Will You Love Me Tomorrow • You've Got a Friend.

00690554 Keyboard Transcriptions.................................$19.95

FOR MORE INFORMATION, SEE YOUR LOCAL MUSIC DEALER, OR WRITE TO:

HAL•LEONARD® CORPORATION

7777 W. BLUEMOUND RD. P.O. BOX 13819 MILWAUKEE, WI 53213

Visit Hal Leonard online at
www.halleonard.com

Prices, contents and availability subject to change without notice.

KEYBOARD STYLE SERIES

These book/CD packs provide focused lessons that contain valuable how-to insight, essential playing tips, and beneficial information for all players. Comprehensive treatment is given to each subject, complete with a companion CD, which features many of the examples in the book performed either solo or with a full band.

BEBOP JAZZ PIANO
THE COMPLETE GUIDE WITH CD!
by John Valerio

In this book, author John Valerio provides essential, detailed information for bebop and jazz keyboardists on the following topics: chords and voicings, harmony and chord progressions, scales and tonality, common melodic figures and patterns, comping, characteristic tunes, the styles of Bud Powell and Thelonious Monk, and much more. The accompanying CD features many of the examples in the book performed either solo or with a full band. Also included are combo performances of five of the tunes featured at the end of the book.
00290535 Book/CD Pack $16.95

BLUES PIANO
THE COMPLETE GUIDE WITH CD!
by Mark Harrison

Blues Piano will teach you the basic skills you need to start playing the blues. From comping to soloing, you'll learn the theory, the tools, and even the tricks that the pros use. You also get seven complete tunes to jam on. Listen to the CD, then start playing along! Covers: scales and chords; left-hand patterns; walking bass; endings and turnarounds; right-hand techniques; how to solo with blues scales; crossover licks; and more.
00311007 Book/CD Pack $16.95

COUNTRY PIANO
THE COMPLETE GUIDE WITH CD!
by Mark Harrison

Learn the basic skills you need to play great country piano. From comping to soloing, you'll learn the theory, the tools, and the tricks used by the pros to get that authentic country sound. At the end of it all, you'll get seven complete tunes to jam on. Listen to the CD, and start playing along! You'll learn: scales and chords, walkup and walkdown patterns, comping in traditional and modern country, Nashville "fretted piano" techniques and more.
00311052 Book/CD Pack $17.95

ROCK KEYBOARD
THE COMPLETE GUIDE WITH CD!
by Scott Miller

Rock Keyboard is chock full of authentic rock keyboard parts. Learn to comp or solo in any of your favorite rock styles. Listen to the CD to hear your parts fit in with the total groove of the band. Includes 99 tracks! Covers: classic rock, pop/rock, blues rock, Southern rock, hard rock, progressive rock, alternative rock, and heavy metal.
00310823 Book/CD Pack $14.95

ROCK 'N' ROLL PIANO
THE COMPLETE GUIDE WITH CD!
by Andy Vinter

With this pack, you'll learn the skills you need to take your place alongside Fats Domino, Jerry Lee Lewis, Little Richard, and other great rock 'n' roll piano players of the '50s and '60s! CD includes demos and backing tracks so you can play along with every example. Also includes six complete tunes at the end of the book! Covers: left-hand patterns; basic rock 'n' roll progressions; right-hand techniques; straight eighths vs. swing eighths; glisses, crushed notes, rolls, note clusters, and more; how to solo; influential players, styles and recordings; and much more!
00310912 Book/CD Pack $14.95

STRIDE & SWING PIANO
THE COMPLETE GUIDE WITH CD!
by John Valerio

Learn the styles of the masters of stride and swing piano, such as Scott Joplin, Jimmy Yancey, Pete Johnson, Jelly Roll Morton, James P. Johnson, Fats Waller, Teddy Wilson, and Art Tatum. This pack covers classic ragtime, early blues and boogie woogie, New Orleans jazz, and more, and includes 14 full songs.
00310882 Book/CD Pack $16.95

Prices, contents, and availability subject to change without notice.

FOR MORE INFORMATION, SEE YOUR LOCAL MUSIC DEALER, OR WRITE TO:

7777 W. BLUEMOUND RD. P.O. BOX 13819 MILWAUKEE, WI 53213

Visit Hal Leonard online at
www.halleonard.com